$3
Low-Sodium
Meals

$3 Low-Sodium Meals

Delicious, Low-Cost Dishes for Your Family That Contain No—or Low—Salt!

Ellen Brown

LYONS PRESS
Guilford, Connecticut

An imprint of Globe Pequot Press

Lyons Press is an imprint of Globe Pequot Press.

Text design: Sheryl P. Kober
Project editor: Julie Marsh
Layout artist: Melissa Evarts

Library of Congress Cataloging-in-Publication Data is available on file.

Brown, Ellen.
  $3 low-sodium meals : delicious, low-cost dishes for your family that contain no- or low- salt / Ellen Brown.
    p. cm.
  Includes index.
  ISBN 978-1-59921-891-5
1. Salt-free diet—Recipes. I. Title. II. Title: Three dollar low-sodium meals.
  RM237.8.B76 2010
  641.5'6323—dc22

Printed in the United States of America

10 9 8 7 6 5 4 3 2 1

Contents

This chapter is your recipe for eating better for less money, even when following a low-sodium diet. Here are all the tips you need to stretch your food budget via strategies for using coupons, shopping sales, and shopping your own pantry.

Cooking a low-sodium diet begins with understanding the role salt plays in our cooking and our eating, as well as learning what foods should be eliminated. This chapter contains that valuable information, in addition to guidance on how to cook beans, make stocks, and bake bread.

Commercial condiments and sauces—from salad dressings and marinades to mayonnaise, mustard, and barbecue sauce—are all loaded with sodium—and they are expensive too. You'll be making delicious low-sodium versions with recipes in this chapter.

A low-sodium way of life extends to some fast and easy dips to enjoy with drinks and some easy and flavorful soups to begin a meal. Those are the dishes you'll be cooking from this collection.

The great news is that fresh vegetables have virtually no sodium! And so many of them are reasonably priced, too. From hearty and thick vegetable stews from around the world to crispy fried patties made from vegetables and beans, there's incredible diversity to the vegetarian dishes in this chapter.

Chapter 6: Aquatic Adventures

Fish is now becoming more available and less expensive, even for land-locked states. The recipes in this chapter are all on the table in merely minutes because fish cooks so quickly, and there are tips for how to prepare batches for future fare.

Chapter 7: Poultry Prowess

The small chicken has eclipsed the large cow in popularity, because of both its relatively lower cost and its solid nutritional profile. The flavorful recipes in this chapter include many ways to cook whole chickens—the most economical way to buy them—along with recipes for the coveted boneless breasts, which are frequently on sale.

Chapter 8: Meaty Matters

Beef has an inherently rich flavor that takes well to countless combinations of seasonings and liquids to make tender beef stews. Pork—"the other white meat"—is gaining popularity in this era of high grocery prices, too, and there are numerous options for roasting it and for stewing it in this chapter.

Chapter 9: Just Desserts

Commercial baked goods, and even homemade treats made with conventional leavening agents, are anathema for a low-sodium diet. But that doesn't mean you won't be having a sweet finale for your meals, including luscious cakes and cookies—some of which are also light.

Preface

I was delighted by the prospect of adding *$3 Low-Sodium Meals* to the series of *$3 Meals* cookbooks. As a food writer, I am constantly following trends in the news linking medical problems and what we eat; there was little question in my mind that reducing sodium in the American diet is clearly necessary.

If the American Medical Association (AMA) believes that more than 150,000 deaths a year can be prevented by switching to a diet low in sodium, I am happy to wave that banner and help make it happen. I've known for years that too much sodium can lead to hypertension, congestive heart failure, and heart attacks. More recently, I learned that postmenopausal women who watch the sodium in their diets are less likely to suffer from osteoporosis because sodium causes calcium to be lost into the urine.

Most of the world's population consumes a diet of between 2,300 mg—the figure recommended in the 2005 Dietary Guidelines for Americans—and 4,600 mg of sodium a day; that's between one and two teaspoons of salt per day. But the *average* American eats a whopping 4,000 mg a day. If that's the average, you know that a lot of people are eating sodium in the range of 6,000 mg a day.

This shows an increase of 55 percent from the early 1970s to 2000. It should not be surprising to learn, therefore, that the prevalence of high blood pressure increased by 50 percent for the same time period.

The AMA's study also confirmed one aspect of the foundation of the *$3 Meals* series: More than 75 percent of the astronomical amount of sodium in the American diet comes from processed foods, including foods eaten at restaurants. These processed foods are also foods that cost more money, so reducing the high cost of food works in tandem with reducing the number of convenience foods that contain chemicals and other unhealthy ingredients—one of which is a high amount of salt.

I'm not going to pick on McDonald's alone, although one small Double Cheeseburger contains 1,150 mg of sodium, which is 48 percent of a daily allowance for someone *not* following a low-sodium diet. We sometimes try to fool ourselves, however, when ordering what we believe is "healthy" fast food. The Roasted Chicken Caesar Salad at KFC has only

530 mg of sodium. Not great, but not too bad. Right? But then there's the dressing at 540 mg per serving and the croutons at 140 mg. So the "healthy" salad lunch contains a whopping 1,210 mg of sodium.

Many Americans are aware of the health hazards posed by the salt, fat, and sugar in fast food meals, but we're less aware of the sodium content in even minimally processed foods such as canned beans and canned tomatoes. These are foods that I regularly used without a concern about their healthfulness. I certainly knew about the chemicals and preservatives in that can of "cream of something soup." But even some reduced-sodium canned chicken stock has more than 600 mg a serving! While I advocate making your own homemade stocks in all *$3 Meals* books as a way to save money, if you're following a low-sodium diet, most of the shelf-stable aisles in the center of the supermarket—including those cans of stocks—are virtually off limits. You'll be in those aisles for foods like pasta, noodles, rice, and dried beans only.

Sodium is everywhere in processed foods, including in a slice of multigrain bread. In fact, a serving of Cheerios contains more sodium than a serving of salted potato chips.

Food manufacturers in the United Kingdom were mandated to reduce the sodium in processed foods by 2010, and New York's Mayor Michael Bloomberg has announced that the city will lead a "nationwide initiative" to pressure the food industry and restaurant chains to halve the salt level in foods over the next decade. But cutting back on salt is up to us until the time that the food industry is forced to get on board.

I understand and appreciate how hard it is to plan healthful meals for your family these days. That's where I can help you and where this book comes in. *$3 Low-Sodium Meals,* as well as the other books in the *$3 Meals* series, is dedicated to helping you produce delicious meals that hide the fact that they're created on a budget and, in this case, keep it a secret that they're actually low in sodium, which makes them good for you.

These recipes will prove to you that low-sodium can still mean high-flavor and that reducing the salt level of foods will never be detected by your family and friends. You will keep everyone healthy while they remain happy, and they'll never even know what you're doing.

Here's the predicament in which we find ourselves. On one side there's the skyrocketing cost of food that challenges all of us who are shopping with a limited food budget. Even if the cost of gasoline drops back, prices at the supermarket will barely change, because the reasons for increasingly expensive food are global and not national. The era when Americans spent a lower percentage of income on food than citizens in other industrialized countries is disappearing as rapidly as drive-in theaters.

For example, converting wheat fields in Umbria to produce sunflowers for ethanol led to a great surge in the price of pasta—a place to which we always turn for the foundation of a low-cost meal—because there's a scarcity of durum wheat. And halfway around the world from this sun-drenched region of Italy, the long-awaited growth of a middle class in both India and China has given Western countries competition for the world's meat supply—and increased the cost of all meats we find in the supermarket.

Then on the other hand is the need to feed yourself and your family meals that are low in sodium and high in nutrients for a healthy life. And you know that nutritionally bankrupt fast food and processed foods are not going to accomplish that aim.

Calculating the sodium content of a dish is a pretty hateful and time-consuming process. But with the recipes in this book, you don't have to bother. They're *all* low-sodium. Karen Konopelski, a registered dietitian who holds a master's degree in the field and has done extensive work on hypertension, worked with me every step of the way. She has also approved any nutritional advice I give you in later chapters.

We all know that many foods that are low in cost are also low in nutrition, as well as being high in sodium. Wearing one hat, you're supposed to be a bargain hunter—a fast and efficient forager—but then you're also asked to spend time reading food labels—and understanding what they mean. Shopping for food could take up a good part of your day! And it can't—because there's too much else to do in this time of scarce money.

There's a cornucopia of inexpensive vegetables in the produce aisle—and in the frozen food aisle—as well as other whole grain and complex carbohydrate foods that are what dietitians praise as being "nutrient dense." Those form the basis for these recipes. But a high percentage of vegetables doesn't mean this is "bunny food"; only a fraction of the contents are vegetarian. Unprocessed meats and fish—you know, the raw stuff—contain relatively little sodium. It's the food processors who are the culprits in changing that nutritional profile.

But don't picture yourself spending hours in the kitchen to make these meals. None requires more than 25 minutes of your time—so the whole working time can be spent listening to the evening news. While many dishes need additional cooking time, you can be doing something else.

Here's the inside scoop on the recipes in this book—diet and denial may start with the same letter, but their similarities end there. These dishes reflect my exuberance for ingredients and for good-tasting foods. I love to cook because I love to eat.

I love herbs and spices and start almost all dishes with at least a few cloves of garlic. (For those of you with family and friends who don't like garlic, add some shallots cooked well.) What I discovered was that without using salt I had to increase the amount of herbs and spices to deliver the same flavor impact. Chile peppers contain almost no sodium, and the addition of an acid such as a mild vinegar or citrus juice can perk your palate in the same way that salt does now.

By cooking the recipes in *$3 Low-Sodium Meals* you'll be ahead of the nutritional curve. Now it's up to the food manufacturers to catch up to you.

Happy eating!

—Ellen Brown
Providence, Rhode Island

Acknowledgments

While writing a book is a solitary endeavor, its publication is a team effort. My thanks go to:

Karen Konopelski, my nutrition consultant, for her knowledge and guidance as well as her skillful analysis of the recipes.

Mary Norris, editorial director at Globe Pequot Press, for so willingly picking up the mantle to serve as editor for this series.

Julie Marsh, project editor at Globe Pequot Press, for her guidance and help all through the production process, and Jessie Shiers for her eagle-eyed copy editing.

Diana Nuhn, senior designer at Globe Pequot Press, for her inspired covers.

Ed Claflin, my agent, for his constant support and great sense of humor.

Tigger and Patches, my furry companions, whose time romping in my office always cheers up my day.

Introduction

My goal is to give you a whole book of recipes that are as satisfying to the taste buds as they are for the food budget, and that are classified as low-sodium, for which the Food and Drug Administration has a clear definition. It's less than 140 mg of sodium per 100 grams (about three ounces) of food. And I wanted to make these dishes so delicious that you won't even look for the now nonexistent salt shaker on the table.

When you figure that the average American diet contains about 4,000 mg of sodium a day, this goal at first seemed unreachable. That was until I saw where all that sodium was coming from. With the exception of the handful of no-salt-added products, mostly in the canned tomato section of the supermarket, every time a processor touches healthful, low-sodium, raw food they add salt to it.

For example, a ½ cup serving of fresh corn contains 12 mg of sodium, while the same size serving of canned corn has a whopping 273 mg. Legumes suffer the same fate when canned; a ½ cup serving of canned black beans, which are cooked, registers 461 mg of sodium, while ½ cup of dried beans—which is actually a lot more beans because they are still dehydrated—has 5 mg.

The more processed the food, the more sodium it contains, along with myriad other chemicals that make reading food labels seem like being back in science class. And the more a food is processed the more expensive it usually becomes because that processing requires machines and the labor to run them.

Back before refrigeration, salting food was a chief method of preserving it. Salt helps to keep food from spoiling by drawing out moisture so bacteria can't grow. Salt also kills existing bacteria that might cause food to spoil.

But spoilage isn't why processed food contains so much sodium today. Salt makes canned soups taste more savory, and it helps to disguise the chemical aftertaste in processed foods made with artificial ingredients. Salt reduces dryness in crackers and pretzels because it causes us to salivate more when eating them, and salt makes cakes and cookies taste sweeter because it unlocks the rest of the taste buds.

Unfortunately, too much sodium in foods is a nasty cycle. As we became more accustomed to eating food with too much sodium, food that had less sodium didn't taste as good. That led manufacturers to increase the sodium level even more, so that a single tablespoon of ketchup contains 190 mg, while the hamburger on which it's placed has far less.

I decided the first step in writing this book was to go on a low-sodium diet myself. I banished the box of sea salt to the pantry and stopped using salt in my cooking. But that was the only change I made, and the food tasted terrible; it was like when you have a cold and nothing tastes good to eat. It lacked flavor.

I then started an intensive study on how our taste buds work and how the sense of taste interacts with our other senses. We really do eat first with our eyes, and then our sense of smell enters the picture. The reason why nothing tastes good if your nose is stuffy is that the aromas from foods cannot tantalize your taste buds prior to their activation from actually tasting the food.

I started cooking with a variety of acids like lemon juice and vinegar, because they jolt the taste buds in the same way as salt. And I started increasing the level of herbs and spices in recipes because without salt to tip off the taste buds, a larger quantity is needed to achieve the same flavor.

You may find, as I did, that it's not easy to follow a low-sodium diet in the beginning. Until your palate adjusts to a lower level of sodium, food just isn't going to taste tasty. But the good news is that studies have shown the adjustment takes place in a matter of days. And that was the case in my own conversion.

Getting going on a low-sodium way of life is not difficult. Here are some tips to help you get started:

Become a human sodium counter. There are countless inexpensive books on the market that contain sodium counts for ingredients as well as brand-name supermarket foods and foods eaten away from home. There's also a wealth of information for free online. Get a source, and familiarize yourself with it.

Start reading food labels. Almost all contain the amount of sodium. Pay attention to the serving size represented by that number. The number of milligrams might seem low, but if the serving size is $1/2$ teaspoon you'll quickly see why.

Keep a food diary. While this does not have to be a permanent part of your life, when starting a low-sodium way of eating it helps you to curb the "mindless munching" that thwarts us all. Write down everything that goes into your mouth, including the cracker you pick up off a coworker's desk or the sample of cookie you ate because they were being given out for free at the supermarket. All those count, and these are all the pitfalls that keeping the diary will point out.

To learn more about healthy eating as advised in the 2005 version of the Dietary Guidelines for Americans from the U.S. Department of Agriculture, visit www.mypyramid.gov. A new version will be released sometime in 2010, and the recommendations may change.

What you'll learn reading—and cooking from—this book is how far your limited food budget can stretch. The goal of *$3 Low-Sodium Meals, as* well as other books in the *$3 Meals* series, is an ambitious one; this small amount of money—less than the cost of a sodium-loaded fast food burger or a slice of gourmet pizza—is for your *whole meal!*

That includes the greens for your tossed salad and the pasta or rice you cook to enjoy all the gravy from a stew. And it includes a sweet treat for dessert. So unlike many books that promise cost-conscious cooking, this book really means it.

These recipes are made with foods that are ingredients; at one time they grew from the earth, walked upon it, or swam in its waters. The most processing that has taken place is the milk of animals being transformed into natural cheeses. So when you're cooking from *$3 Low-Sodium Meals,* you're satisfying your body as well as your budget.

Not only for your body, but also for the planet, it is beneficial to use organic ingredients whenever possible. While organics used to be priced higher than conventional products, that is no longer the case. Most major supermarket chains, and mass retailers such as Wal-Mart, now carry extensive lines of organic ingredients, both fresh and shelf-stable. So buying organic is now a choice open to all—regardless of food budget.

The term was vague until 2001 when the U.S. Department of Agriculture set standards that clearly defined the meaning of *organic* both in terms of the food and the farming practices.

Organic agriculture prohibits the use of most synthetic fertilizers and pesticides, sewer sludge fertilizers, genetic engineering, growth hormones, irradiation, antibiotics, and artificial ingredients. In modern times antioxidants in our bodies have had to work even harder to combat the ravages of environmental pollutants, and organic farming does not add to those factors.

When the word *organic* is used in relation to meats, eggs, and dairy products, it means that the animals have not been given drugs or growth hormones, and they have been kept in conditions that allow for regular exercise and humane treatment.

In terms of saving the earth, the agricultural practices used for organic farming are environmentally friendly. Soil fertility and crop nutrient management must be done to improve soil conditions, minimize erosion, and prevent contamination of crops. Farmers must use crop rotation methods and fertilize with composted animal manure and plant materials rather than chemicals. Pests are controlled by traps rather than chemical sprays, and plastic mulches are forbidden.

In these recipes there are a few ingredient compromises taken to trim costs; however, these shortcuts trim preparation time, too. For my series of *$3 Meals* books, I've used bottled lemon and lime juice in recipe development rather than freshly squeezed juices from the fruits themselves; I discovered it took a bit more juice to achieve the flavor I was after, but with the escalated cost of citrus fruits, this was a sacrifice that I chose to make.

The same is true with vegetables; many of these recipes call for cost-effective frozen vegetables rather than fresh. For vegetables such as the chopped spinach added to a soup or casserole, or the peas added to many dishes, it really doesn't matter. Unlike canned vegetables, the sodium content of frozen vegetables is about the same as fresh vegetables, and they can save considerable money as well as time.

I've also limited the range of herbs and spices specified to a core group of fewer than a dozen. There's no need to purchase an expensive dried herb that you may never use again. If you grow fresh herbs, please feel free to substitute them at the rate of 1 tablespoon of a chopped fresh herb for each 1 teaspoon of a dried herb. While I adore fresh herbs, a small bunch in most supermarkets is double the cost of a dozen eggs—and that can serve as the protein for six people's dinner.

On the other hand, there are standards I will never bend. I truly believe that unsalted butter is so far superior to margarine that any minimal cost savings or savings of saturated fat grams from using margarine is not worth the trade-down in flavor.

And flavor is what these recipes are all about. It may take you a few weeks of low-sodium eating to have your palate adjust to the healthier and lower levels in your food, but then you'll be tasting those natural flavors more strongly.

A quick housekeeping detail before you start cooking these recipes. The nutritional analysis given is for each recipe as written, and not for the variations. While none of the variations will substantially alter the analysis, because none of the ingredients suggested are high in sodium, the actual count may not be the same. The analysis also does not include items such as rice on which the food is to be served.

Chapter 1:
Saving Money at the Supermarket

Trimming money from your grocery bill is important, regardless of what you're cooking. The recipes in this book will help you to eat a healthful, low-sodium diet that is delicious as well as economical, but my help starts here in this chapter.

As you can well imagine, as a cookbook author I spend a lot of time in supermarkets, as well as other venues—from picturesque farmers' markets to the food aisles of chain drug stores—that sell food. One thing is certain—every other customer I talk to is as interested as you are and I am to eat better on a limited food budget. Those are the strategies you'll learn in this chapter.

Think of plotting and planning your supermarket trips as if you were planning to take the kids on a vacation. Your first step is to decide on your destination—what supermarket or other stores you'll use. After that you buy some guidebooks (in this case the Sunday newspaper) and do other research online (like print out coupons), and then you start looking for the good deals to get you to where you want to go.

In this case, where you want to go is to treat yourself to a vacation, and the way you're going to afford it in these challenging economic times is by savvy shopping. At any given moment there are *billions* of dollars of grocery coupons in the world waiting to be redeemed. Unfortunately, a large percentage of coupons are for processed foods, which are high in sodium, so won't be part of your list. But if you really don't care that much about the brand of toothpaste, laundry detergent, or yogurt you eat, there are ways to save money every week.

In addition to coupons, there are rebates; if you spend a few cents on a stamp, it could reap many dollars coming back from manufacturers. They usually throw in some extra coupons, too.

Most of the tips are specific to food shopping; this *is* a cookbook. But there are also hints for saving money in other segments of your budget. It's all coming out of the same wallet.

I wish I could promise you a clear and uncluttered path. But every rule has an exception, as you'll see below. You're now turning shopping from a simple ritual into a complex task. But the results are worth the effort you'll be putting in.

PLAN *BEFORE* YOU SHOP

The most important step to cost-effective cooking is to decide logically and intelligently what you're going to cook for the week. That may sound simple, but if you're in the habit of deciding as you leave work at the end of the day, chances are you've ended up with a lot of frozen pizza or Chinese carry-out. Changing from impromptu eating to a well-crafted plan is also the foundation of maintaining your low-sodium diet; you need to cook with real ingredients to cut back on sodium rather than eating processed food.

The first step is to "shop" in a place you know well; it's your own kitchen. Look and see what's still in the refrigerator, and how that food—which you've already purchased and perhaps also cooked—can be utilized.

Now look at what foods you have in the freezer. Part of savvy shopping is stocking up on foods when they're on sale; in fact, sales of free-standing freezers have grown by more than 10 percent during the past few years, while sales of all other major appliances have gone down. And with good reason—a free-standing freezer allows you to take advantage of sales. Especially foods like boneless, skinless chicken breasts—the time-crunched cook's best friend—that go on sale frequently and are almost prohibitive in price when they're not on sale. In addition, you need room in a freezer for the packets of beans and containers of no-salt-added stocks you'll be learning to cook in Chapter 2.

But preparing food for the freezer to ensure its future quality is important. Never freeze meats, poultry, or seafood in the supermarket wrapping alone. To guard against freezer burn, double wrap food in freezer paper or place it in a heavy resealable plastic bag. Mark the purchase date on raw food, and the date the food was frozen on cooked items, and use them within three months.

Most supermarkets have a lower cost for buying larger quantities, and by freezing part of a package you can take advantage of that savings. Scan recipes and look at the amount of the particular meat specified; that's what size your packages destined for the freezer should be. A good investment is a kitchen scale to weigh portions, if you don't feel comfortable judging weight freestyle.

Keep a list taped to the front of your freezer. It should list contents and date when each item was frozen. Mark off foods as you take them out and add foods as you put them in.

Also, part of your strategy as a cook is actually to cook only a few nights a week or on one day of a weekend; that means when you're making recipes that can be doubled—like soups and stews—you make larger batches and freeze a portion. Those meals are "dinner insurance" for nights you don't want to cook. Those are the nights that you previously would have brought in the bucket of chicken or the high-priced rotisserie chicken, and spent far more money and eaten far more sodium.

The other factor that enters into the initial planning is looking at your depletion list, and seeing what foods and other products need to be purchased. A jar of peanut butter or a bottle of dishwashing liquid might not factor into meal plans, but they do cost money—so they have to be factored into your budget. Some weeks you might not need many supplies, but it always seems to me that all of the cleaning supplies seem to deplete the same week.

Now you've got the "raw data" to look at the weekly sales circulars from your newspaper or delivered with your mail. Those sales, along with online research to accrue even more money-saving coupons, should form the core for your menu planning.

COUPON CLIPPING 101

It's part art, it's part science, and it all leads to more money in your wallet. Consider this portion of the chapter your Guerilla Guide to Coupons. There's more to it than just clipping them. Of course, unless you clip them or glean them from other channels (see some ideas below) then you can't save money. So that's where you're going to start—but, trust me, it's just the beginning.

Forget that image you have of the lady wearing the hairnet and the "sensible shoes" in line at the supermarket digging through what seems to be a bottomless pit of tiny pieces of paper looking for the right coupon for this or that. Clipping coupons—in case you haven't heard—is *cool*.

And it should be. At any given moment there are *billions of dollars* of coupons floating around out there, according to the folks at www .grocerycouponguide.com, one of the growing list of similar sites dedicated to helping you save money.

Not only is it becoming easier to access these savings, you're a Neanderthal if you don't. The fact that you're reading this book—and will be cooking from it—shows that you care about trimming the size of your grocery bill. So it's time to get with the program.

Coupon usage grew by a whopping 192 percent in the year between March of 2008 and March of 2009, according to Coupons.com, which has seen an increase of 25 percent per month since the current recession began.

Even the Sunday newspaper (as long as they still exist) is a treasure-trove of coupons. I found a $5 off coupon for a premium cat food my finicky cats liked in a local paper, which cost 50 cents. It was worth it to buy four copies of the paper; I spent $2 but I then netted an $18 savings on the cat food.

The Internet is increasingly a place to turn for coupons, both a few dollars here and there on groceries and many dollars off for major purchases like computers or televisions. Stores like Target frequently have coupons for up to 10 percent off an order, too.

Here are some good sites to browse. For many coupons you have to download some free software to print them off; it's worth the few minutes of your time:

- www.GroceryCoupons.com

- www.CouponMom.com

- www.GroceryGuide.com

- www.PPGazette.com

- www.GroceryCoupons4U.com

LEARNING THE LINGO

Coupons are printed on very small pieces of paper, and even with 20/20 eyesight or reading glasses many people—including me—need to use a magnifying glass to read all the fine print. There are many legal phrases that have to be part of every coupon, too.

In the same way that baseball fans know that RBI means "runs batted in," coupon collectors know that WSL means "while supplies last." Here's a list of many abbreviations found on coupons:

AR. After rebate.

B1G1 or **BOGO.** Buy one, get one free.

CRT. Cash register tape, also called your receipt.

While you may be just becoming more aware of them, coupons are nothing new. They began in the late 1800s when Coca-Cola and Grape Nuts offered coupons to consumers. Currently more than 3,000 companies use coupons as part of their marketing plans, and shoppers save more than $5 billion a year by redeeming the coupons.

DC. Double coupon, which is a coupon the store—not the manufacturer—doubles in value.

DCRT. Dated cash register receipt, which proves you purchased the item during the right time period.

FAR. Free after rebate.

IP. Internet printed coupons.

ISO. In-store only.

IVC. Instant value coupon, which are the pull offs found on products in the supermarket that are redeemed as you pay.

MIR. Mail-in rebate.

NED. No expiration date.

OAS. On any size, which means the coupon is good for any size package of that particular product.

OYNSO. On your next shopping order, which means that you must return to the same store; the coupon will not be good at another store.

POP. Proof of purchase, which is the little panel found on a package that you cut out and send in to receive a rebate.

WSL. While supplies last, which means you can't demand a "rain check" to use the coupon at a later date when the product is once again in stock.

GET ORGANIZED!

So you now have a fistful of coupons with which you're going to save money at the supermarket. That's a start; if you don't have the coupons you can't use them.

The first decision you have to make is how you're going to organize your coupons. There are myriad ways and each has its fans. It's up to you to decide which is right for you, your family, and the way you shop:

- **Arrange the coupons by aisle in the supermarket.** This is only good if you shop in one store consistently.

- **Arrange the coupons by category of product.** Dairy products, cleaning supplies, paper disposables, and cereals are all categories with many weekly coupons, so arrange your coupons accordingly.

- **Arrange the coupons alphabetically.** This system works well if you redeem coupons in various types of stores beyond the grocery store.

- **Arrange the coupons by expiration date.** Coupons are only valid for a certain time period; it can be a few weeks or a few months. And part of the strategy of coupon clipping is to maximize the value, which frequently comes close to the expiration date. Some of the best coupons are those for "buy one, get one free." However, when the coupon first appears the item is at full price. But what about two weeks later when the item is on sale at your store? Then the "buy one, get one free" can mean you're actually getting four cans for the price of one at the original retail price.

Storage systems for arranging coupons are as varied as methods of organizing them. I personally use envelopes, and keep the stack held together with a low-tech paper clip. I've also seen people with whole wallets and tiny accordion binders dedicated to coupons. If you don't have a small child riding on the top of the cart, another alternative is to get a loose-leaf notebook with clear envelopes instead of pages.

Sometimes coupons expire *before* their stated expiration date because retailers allot so many dollars per promotion. If, for example, a retailer is offering a free widget if you buy a widget holder, and the widgets run out, there's probably a way to justify turning you away. Read the fine print.

BARGAIN SHOPPING 2.0

Every grocery store has weekly sales, and those foods are the place to start your planning for new purchases; that's how you're saving money beyond using coupons. And almost every town has competing supermarket chains that offer different products on sale. It's worth your time to shop in a few venues, because it will generate the most savings. That way you can also determine which chain offers the best store brands, and purchase them while you're there for the weekly bargains. As I said before, your options are more limited because you won't be buying any high-sodium processed foods, but it's more than worth your time to use every trick in the book to trim that grocery budget. Here are other ways to save:

- **Shuffle those cards.** Even if I can't convince you to clip coupons, the least you can do for yourself to save money is take the five minutes required to sign up for store loyalty cards; many national brands as well as store brands are on sale only when using the card. While the current system has you hand the card to the cashier at the checkout, that will be changing in the near future. Shopping carts will be equipped with card readers that will generate instant coupons according to your purchasing habits. I keep my stack of loyalty cards in the glove box of my car; that way they don't clutter my purse but I always have them when shopping.

- **Segregate items not on your list.** Some of these might be marked down meats or vegetables, and some might be impulse buys that end up in the cart despite your pledge to keep to the list. Place these items in the "baby rack" rather than in the cart; you'll have a good visual sense of how much money is represented.

- **"Junk mail" may contain more than junk.** Don't toss those Valpak and other coupon envelopes that arrive in the mail. Look through them carefully, and you'll find not only coupons for food products, but for many services, too.

- **Look for blanket discounts.** While it does take time to cull coupons, many supermarket chains send flyers in the mail that offer a set amount off the total, for example $10 off a total of $50. These are the easiest way to save money, and many national drug store chains, such as CVS, do the same. Just remember to have a loyalty card for those stores to take advantage of the savings.

- **Spend a stamp to get a rebate.** Despite the current cost of a first-class postage stamp, sending in for rebates is still worth your trouble. Many large manufacturers are now sending out coupon books or cash vouchers usable in many stores to customers who mail in receipts demonstrating that they have purchased about $50 of products. For example, Procter & Gamble, the country's largest advertiser and the company for which the term "soap opera" was invented, is switching millions of dollars from the airwaves to these sorts of promotions.

- **Find bargains online.** There are some specific coupon sites listed above, but there are other places to look, too. Go to specific manufacturers of foods you like, even high-end organic foods. You'll find coupons as well as redemption offers. I also look for the coupon offers on such culinary sites as www.epicurious.com and www.foodnetwork.com. You will find coupons there, some tied to actual recipes.

- **Find coupons in the store.** Look for those little machines projecting from the shelves; they usually contain coupons that can be used instantly when you check out. Also, don't throw out your receipt until you've looked at it carefully. There are frequently coupons printed on the back. The cashier may also hand you other small slips of paper with your cash register receipt; most of them are coupons for future purchases of items you just bought. They may be from the same brand or they may be from a competing brand. Either way, they offer savings.

- **Stock up on cans.** You'll be using few canned goods and other shelf-stable foods because of their high sodium count, but if a brand of no-salt-added tomato products is on sale, jump on it. The same plastic containers that fit under your bed to hold out-of-season clothing can also become a pantry for canned goods.

- **Get a bargain buddy.** There's no question that supermarkets try to lure customers with "buy one, get one free" promotions, and sometimes one is all you really want. And those massive cases of paper towels at the warehouse clubs are also a good deal—if you have unlimited storage space. The answer? Find a bargain buddy with whom you can split large purchases. My friends and I also swap coupons we won't use but the other person will. Going back to my example of the cat food savings, there were dog food coupons on the same page, so I turned them over to a canine-owning friend.

PUSHING THE CART WITH PURPOSE

So it's a "new you" entering the supermarket. First of all, you have a list, and it's for more than a few days. And you're going to buy what's on your list. Here's the first rule: stick to that list. Never go shopping when you're hungry; that's when non-essential treats high in sodium wind up in your basket.

Always go shopping alone; unwanted items end up in the cart to keep peace in the family. And—here's an idea that might seem counter-intuitive—go shopping when you're in a hurry. It's those occasions when you have the time to dawdle that the shortcakes end up coming home when all you really wanted were the strawberries.

But, as promised, here are some exceptions to the rule of keeping to your list. You've got to be flexible enough to take advantage of some unexpected, great sales. Next to frugality, flexibility is the key to saving money on groceries.

It's easy if the sale is a markdown on meat; you see the $2 off coupon and put it in the cart, with the intention of either cooking it that night or freezing it. All supermarkets mark down meat on the day before the expiration date. The meat is still perfectly fine, and should it turn out not to be, you can take it back for a refund. So go ahead and take advantage of the markdown.

Then you notice a small oval sticker with the word "Save." Is turkey breast at $1.09 a real bargain? You'll know it is if you keep track of prices and remember that a few weeks ago it was $3.99 per pound.

You now have two options. Buy the off-list bargains and freeze them, or use them this week. In place of what? And what effect will that have on the rest of your list?

That's why I suggest freezing bargains, assuming you can absorb the extra cost on this week's grocery bill. If not, then look at what produce and dairy items on the list were tied to a protein you're now crossing off, and delete them too.

But meat isn't the only department of the supermarket that has "remainder bins." Look for produce too. I've gotten some perfectly ripe bananas with black spots—just the way they should be—for pennies a pound, while the ones that are bright yellow (and still tasteless) are five times the cost.

Supermarkets are almost all designed to funnel traffic first into the produce section; that is actually the last place you want to shop. Begin with the proteins, since many items in other sections of your list relate to the entrees of the dinners you have planned. Once they are gathered, go through and get the pasta, rice, or other low-sodium shelf-stable items, then the dairy products (so they will not be in the cart for too long) and end with the produce. Using this method, the fragile produce is on the top of the basket, not crushed by the gallons of milk.

The last step is packing the groceries. If you live in an area where you have the option of packing them yourself, place items stored together in the same bag. That way all of your produce can go directly into the refrigerator, and canned goods destined for the basement will be stored in one trip.

LEARNING THE ROPES

The well-informed shopper is the shopper who is saving money, and the information you need to make the best purchasing decision is right there on the supermarket shelves. It's the shelf tag that gives you the cost per unit of measurement. The units can be quarts for salad dressing, ounces for dry cereal, or pounds for canned goods. All you have to do is look carefully.

But you do have to make sure you're comparing apples to apples and oranges to oranges—or in this example, stocks to stocks. Some can be priced by the quart, while others are by the pound.

- **Check out store brands.** Store brands and generics have been improving in quality during the past few years, and according to *Consumer Reports,* buying them can save anywhere from 15 percent to 50 percent. Moving from a national brand to a store brand is a personal decision, and sometimes money is not the only factor. For example, I have used many store brands of chlorine bleach, and have returned to Clorox time and again. But I find no difference between generic shredded wheat, a very low-sodium cereal, and those from the market leaders. Store brands can also be less expensive than national brands on sale—and with coupons.

- **Compare prices within the store.** Many foods—such as cold cuts and cheeses—are sold in multiple areas of the store, so check out those alternate locations. Sliced ham may be less expensive in a cellophane package shelved with the refrigerated foods than at the deli counter.

- **Look high and low.** Manufacturers pay a premium price to shelve products at eye level, and you're paying for that placement when you're paying their prices. Look at the top and bottom shelves in aisles like cleaning products and pasta. That's where you'll find the lower prices.

- **Buy the basics.** Remember that any time a person other than you is working on food, you're paying for that labor cost. You'll learn how to cut up your own chickens in Chapter 7, and maybe it takes a few minutes to turn those carrots into carrot sticks, but it's a lot cheaper than buying baby carrots, and you'll have the peels that can flavor your stocks.

- **Watch the scanner.** I know it's tempting to catch up on pop culture by leafing through the tabloids at the checkout, but that's the last thing you should be doing—and that's another reason to go shopping without the kids because they will be a distraction. Watching the clerk scan your order usually saves you money. For example, make sure all the instant savings coupons are peeled off; this includes marked-down meats and coupons on boxes and bags. Then, make sure sale items are ringing up at the right price.

WASTE NOT, WANT NOT

We're now going to start listing exceptions to all the rules you just read, because a bargain isn't a bargain if you end up throwing some of it away. Remember that the goal is to waste nothing. Start by annotating your shopping list with quantities for the recipes you'll be cooking. That way you can begin to gauge when a bargain is a bargain. Here are other ways to buy only what you need:

- **Don't overbuy.** Sure, the large can of diced tomatoes is less per pound than the smaller can. But what will you do with the remainder of the can if all you need is a small amount? The same is true for dairy products. A half-pint of heavy cream always costs much more per ounce than a quart, but if the remaining three cups of cream will end up in the sink in a few weeks, go with the smaller size.

- **Buy what you'll eat, not what you *should* eat.** Ah, this is where parental guilt comes into play. You've just read an article on the wonders of broccoli, and there it is on sale. But if your family hates broccoli, the low sale cost doesn't matter; you'll end up throwing it away. We all think about healthful eating when we're in the supermarket, but if you know that the contents of your cart are good thoughts rather than realistic choices, you're wasting money.

- **Just because you have a coupon doesn't mean you should buy something.** We all love bargains, but if you're putting an item into your cart for the first time, you must decide if it's because you really want it and haven't bought it before because of its cost, or because you're getting $1.50 off of the price. This is a subset of buying what you eat, and not what you should eat.

- **Sometimes bigger isn't better.** If you're shopping for snacks for your kids, look for the *small* apples rather than the giant ones. Most kids take a few bites and then toss the rest, so evaluate any purchases you're making by the pound.

- **Ring that bell!** You know the one; it's always in the meat department of the supermarket. It might take you a few extra minutes, but ask the real live human who will appear for *exactly* what you want; many of the recipes in *$3 Low-Sodium* specify less than the weight of packages you find in the meat case. Many supermarkets do not have personnel readily available in departments like the cheese counter, but if there are wedges of cheeses labeled and priced, then someone is in charge. It might be the deli department or the produce department, but find out who it is and ask for a small wedge of cheese if you can't find one that's cut to the correct size. You won't be eating very much cheese because it contains a lot of sodium, so don't let it go to waste.

- **Check out the bulk bins.** Begin buying from the bulk bins for shelf-stable items, like various types of rice, beans, dried fruits, and unsalted nuts. Each of these departments has scales so you can weigh ingredients like dried mushrooms or pasta. If a recipe calls for a quantity rather than a weight, you can usually "eyeball" the quantity. If you're unsure of amounts, start by bringing a 1-cup measuring cup with you to the market. Empty the contents of the bin into the measuring cup rather than directly into the bag. One problem with bulk food bags is that they are difficult to store in the pantry; shelves were made for sturdier materials. Wash out plastic deli containers or even plastic containers that you bought containing yogurt or sour cream. Use those for storage once the bulk bags arrive in the kitchen. Make sure you label your containers of bulk foods both at the supermarket and at home (if you're transferring the foods to other containers) so you know what they are, especially if you're buying similar foods. Arborio and basmati rice look very similar in a plastic bag, but they are totally different grains and shouldn't be substituted for each other.

- **Shop from the salad bar for tiny quantities.** There's no question that supermarkets charge a premium price for items in those chilled bins in the salad bar, but you get exactly what you need. When to shop there depends on the cost of the item in a larger quantity. If you don't see how you're going to finish the $4 pint of cherry tomatoes, then spend $1 at the salad bar for the handful you need to garnish a salad. And if you're not crazy about celery, get the 1/2 cup you need from the salad bar rather than buying a whole stalk for a few dollars.

SUPERMARKET ALTERNATIVES

All of the hints thus far in this chapter have been geared to pushing a cart around a supermarket. Here are some other ways to save money:

- **Shop at farmers' markets.** I admit it; I need a 12-step program to help me cure my addiction to local farmers' markets. Shopping alfresco on warm summer days turns picking out fruits and vegetables into a truly sensual experience. Also, you buy only what you want. There are no bunches of carrots; there are individual carrots sold by the pound. The U.S. Department of Agriculture began publishing the *National Directory of Farmers' Markets* in 1994, and at that time the number was fewer than 2,000. That figure has now doubled. To find a farmers' market near you, go to www.ams.usda.gov/farmersmarkets. The first cousins of farmers' markets for small quantities of fruits are the sidewalk vendors in many cities. One great advantage to buying from them is that their fruit is always ripe and ready to eat or cook.

- **Shop at ethnic markets.** If you live in a rural area this may not be possible, but even moderately small cities have a range of ethnic markets, and that's where you should buy ingredients to cook those cuisines. The vegetables are frequently less expensive. Even small cities and many towns have ethnic enclaves, such as a "Little Italy"; each neighborhood has some grocery stores with great prices for those ingredients and the fresh produce used to make the dishes, too.

- **Shop alternative stores.** Groceries aren't only at grocery stores; many "dollar stores" and other discount venues stock herbs and spices as well as pasta and rice. If you live in New England, Ocean State Job Lot should be on your weekly circuit; this discount store chain is loaded with food bargains.

- **Shop for food in drug stores.** Every national brand of drugstore—including CVS and Walgreen's—carries grocery products, and usually has great bargains each week. In the same way that food markets now carry much more than foods, drug stores stock thousands of items that have no connection to medicine. Those chains also have circulars in Sunday newspapers, so check them out—even if you're feeling very healthy.

- **Shop online.** In recent years it's become possible to do all your grocery shopping online through such services as Peapod and Fresh Express. While there is frequently a delivery charge involved, for housebound people this is a true boon. If you really hate the thought of pushing the cart, you should explore it; it's impossible to make impulse buys. There are also a large number of online retailers for ethnic foods, dried herbs and spices, premium baking chocolate, and other shelf-stable items. Letting your cursor do the shopping for these items saves you time, and many of them offer free shipping at certain times of the year.

TIME FOR MENTAL CALISTHENICS

Just as an athlete goes through mental preparation before a big game, getting yourself "psyched" to save money is the first step to accomplishing that goal. You've got to get into a frugal frame of mind. You're out to save money on your food budget, but not feel deprived. You're going to be eating the delicious dishes in this book.

Think about where your food budget goes other than the grocery store. The cost of a few "designer coffee" treats at the local coffee shop is equal to a few dinners at home. Couldn't you brew coffee and take it to work rather than spend $10 a week at the coffee cart? And those cans of soft drinks in the vending machine are four times the cost of bringing a can from home. But do you really need soft drinks at all? For mere pennies you can brew a few quarts of iced tea, which is lower in sugar than soft drinks and has delicious flavor without chemicals.

Planning ahead is important, too. Rather than springing for a chilled bottle of spring water because you're thirsty in the supermarket, keep a few empty plastic bottles in your car and fill one from the water fountain. That water is free.

Until frugality comes naturally, do what diet counselors suggest, and keep a log of every penny spent on food. Just as the empty calories add up, so do the meaningless noshes. And most of the time what you're nibbling isn't on a low-sodium diet.

Bringing your lunch to work does increase your weekly supermarket tab, but it accomplishes a few good goals. It adds funds to the bottom line of your total budget, and it allows you to control what you're eating—and when.

If you have a pressured job, chances are there are days that you end up eating from snack food vending machines or eating fast food at your desk. If you're following a low-sodium diet, it's imperative to bring your lunch so you know what it will be—even if you don't know when you'll be eating it.

Almost every office has both a refrigerator and a microwave oven, so lunch can frequently be a leftover from a dinner the night or two before, so the extra cost and cooking time are minimal.

Frugality also extends to saving your old bags if you shop at a store that gives you 5 cents off your order for each of your own bags you use. While 5 cents doesn't seem like much, it will put a few dollars into your pocket over a year's time. And you're helping the environment, too, because less packaging is ending up in landfills; the environmental term for it is "source reduction."

So now that you're becoming a grocery guru, you can move on to find myriad ways to save money on your grocery bill while eating wonderfully. That's what *$3 Low-Sodium Meals,* and the other books in the *$3 Meals* series, is all about.

Chapter 2:
Shaking the Shaker

Low-sodium cooking does take more time because you can't rely on processed food. There will be times, until you get into the routine of low-sodium cooking, that you'll feel you've returned to Grandma's era. And with good reason. All those cans and packages you've been using to make cooking more convenient are the ones that are now banished from your shopping basket because they're so high in sodium.

You're going to have to cook beans from a package of dried beans rather than opening up an inexpensive can. But you can flavor the beans, too, and using a slow cooker you don't have to watch over them.

I hope you'll find that there are great benefits to this return to yesteryear. Once you've gotten into the habit of making stocks for soups and sauces yourself, you'll wonder why you ever spent money on those sodium-filled cans and boxes because the flavor is so much richer, *and* you're saving money.

Breads are where a lot of people on low-sodium diets draw the line; it's just too much trouble to make them yourself. But I included some recipes for them at the end of this chapter because a crusty loaf of French bread or a focaccia coming from the oven with the aroma of herbs and garlic is really easy to make. And making them is far less expensive than buying them.

Those are the sorts of recipes you'll find in this chapter, along with some general information on how your taste buds function and foods to avoid when following a low-sodium diet.

Always keep in mind that sodium is necessary for a person to be healthy. It serves to keep the fluids balanced correctly in the body, and it helps the muscles in your body to relax and contract. But it takes very little sodium to accomplish these tasks.

TRICKING YOUR TASTE BUDS
We tend to take our senses, including the sense of taste, for granted, but they are as biologically complex as any system in our bodies can be. To understand how to reduce the amount of sodium in your diet, it helps to understand how taste and taste buds work.

Taste buds are chemoreceptors, which means they translate the chemical signals they get from food into electrical signals that travel to the brain using the nervous system. The old biology map of the mouth showing your tongue and what receptors are located where has been revised in recent years.

Most scientists now think there are five, rather than four, distinct types of taste buds; the traditional ones of salty, sweet, bitter, and sour are now joined by one termed "umami," which is savory. Researchers also believe that the ability to sense each of these five tastes is located all over the mouth, not just on the tongue.

In general, humans think of salty, sweet, and savory foods as pleasant, and sour and bitter foods as unpleasant. Sour and bitter could be signs that food is rotten or poisoned, so detecting those tastes was important for survival.

While there is still some controversy in the scientific community regarding umami, there is total agreement that the other four types of taste buds exist. When you chew, the food is dissolved by the saliva and enters the taste bud through a pore in its center. When food comes in contact with the taste buds, a message is sent to your brain. The brain computes these signals, along with aroma and texture, to cause you to recognize different tastes.

While salty taste buds frequently trigger the other taste buds to open up as well, their first cousin in that regard are the sour taste buds. That's why so many of the recipes in *$3 Low-Sodium Meals* contain some sort of acid such as citrus juice, wine, vinegar, or tomatoes.

A molecule of table salt, chemically called sodium chloride (NaCl), contains a positively charged sodium ion and a negatively charged chlorine ion. The sodium ions trigger ion channels in the taste buds, changing the electrical charge of the taste bud cells and beginning the potential for further action. In the same way, sour foods containing acid contain positively charged hydrogen ions that create the action potential in the taste buds. That's why just eliminating the salt from your cooking makes foods taste bland; the sodium needs some sort of acid to take its place.

Another theory on the role of sodium taste buds, published by Paul Breslin of the prestigious Monell Chemical Senses Center in Philadelphia, is that salt suppresses bitter tastes and accentuates sweet flavors.

An additional way to turn on the taste buds is with foods that actually cause a chemical irritation. The capsaicin in chile peppers, the gingerols in ginger, the piperin in black pepper, and the wide range of compounds in onion, mustard, garlic, radishes, and horseradish all cause a chemical reaction that makes us think "hot." These foods actually stimulate pain fibers that are similar to the ones that warn us off of sipping a cup of boiling coffee. We regard them as "hot" foods, and these chemical reactions turn on the taste buds.

How these irritating foods work on our brains is still being studied. One study conducted about 30 years ago by Dr. Paul Rozin at the University of Pennsylvania presents the theory that these foods create the release of endorphins, the same neurochemicals responsible for the euphoria of the famed "runner's high."

How many of these chemically irritating foods a person can tolerate, or wants to tolerate, changes individually. Part of the reaction is due to genetics, but also to a gradual desensitization to the chemicals. It's this state of lowered sensation that leads to natives of countries where dishes are loaded with chiles and other irritating foods to be able to eat them with barely a tear forming.

Keep in mind that the taste buds are hardly acting alone. We eat first with our eyes, which is why people become turned off by the sight of a favorite food—be it a steak or a bowl of strawberries—if it is illuminated by a light that makes it appear to be of another color. Then there's the smell test. Don't you always give a sniff to a leftover you don't remember putting into the refrigerator, even if it looks good? One whiff and you start heading for the garbage can, even if your eyes haven't sent the danger message.

The steam from hot food travels into your nasal passages, and once you start chewing the food the aromas start traveling to your nose through the back of the throat.

While there are many scientific theories surrounding why we eat what we eat, and why we like what we eat, there is also a sociological theory, which is that the more we eat a food, the more we like it. So if you're accustomed to eating sodium-loaded processed food, that is your expectation. Once your body and your mind have adjusted to cooking with fresh ingredients that are low in sodium, those will replace processed foods as your point of reference.

Replacing the bag of chips with the bowl of berries will not happen overnight. But it will happen.

FOODS TO FORGET

As you now know, if you're following a low-sodium diet, or want to reduce the sodium in the foods you cook at home to combat the sodium in processed foods you eat away from home, there are certain foods that will become memories, or treats to savor on an occasional basis.

As a general rule, avoid three key areas of the supermarket—the center aisles of shelf-stable foods, the deli department, and the bakery department. These are the "red light districts" for high-sodium choices. It's a good general rule that if it's shelf-stable, and it doesn't say "No Salt Added" in big letters on the label, it's not for you. In particular, here's a list of specific danger zones:

- Anchovies and other canned fish such as tuna, salmon, and sardines. Examine cans of low-sodium tuna carefully; there is a large variation in the amount of sodium among brands.

- Asian food in general because the prevalent seasonings, such as soy sauce and fish sauce *(nam pla),* are all very high in sodium.

- Bacon, ham, and any type of prepared sausage products, including hot dogs or anything that comes in a link.

- Baked goods, both packaged and from a bakery or bakery department of the supermarket. Most contain baking soda and baking powder, both of which are sky high in sodium. Even commercial yeast breads are fairly high; most are a few hundred milligrams a slice.

- Buttermilk contains much more sodium than fresh milk, and you can make your own soured milk by adding 2 tablespoons lemon juice to each cup of milk.

- Most cheeses, except in very small portions, such as Swiss cheese and Parmesan cheese.

- Cold cereals and instant hot cereals can be culprits; look at the packages carefully. While two whole big shredded wheat biscuits only have 3 milligrams of sodium, a cup of Wheat Chex cereal has 267 milligrams. As with other food categories, figure that if someone is processing the food, or augmenting its flavor with sugar, they're also adding salt.

- Cold cuts of any type, including corned beef, pastrami, and any Italian cold cuts.

- Condiments as a food category are very high in sodium, including ketchup, mustard, mayonnaise, cocktail sauce, prepared salad dressings, steak sauce, Worcestershire sauce, hot red pepper sauce (use crushed red pepper flakes or fresh chiles instead), and prepared horseradish. You'll find a lot of low-sodium condiment recipes in Chapter 3 of this book for that reason.

- Frozen foods, except for frozen vegetables not packed in any sort of sauce. While that frozen entree boasts its low calories, the front of the box never mentions the sodium content for a good reason.

- Olives because both the brine- and oil-cured types are cured with a lot of salt.

- Pickles and pickled foods like sauerkraut and relish.

- Salted snacks such as tortilla chips, potato chips, and pretzels.

- Seasoning blends unless they say "no salt added," and any mixes for soups and sauces.

- Smoked fish of any kind. To give you an example, a 3-ounce portion of fresh salmon has 50 milligrams of sodium, while the same size portion of smoked salmon has 666 milligrams. And smoked fish is expensive, too.

- Vegetables in cans, including beans and tomatoes. Look only for cans marked "no salt added."

READING IT RIGHT

Although it does take some time, it's good training when you're first starting on the road to low-sodium cooking to read the nutritional labels on anything you're putting into your shopping cart. Factor this time into your shopping trips, but after two or three label-looking trips, you'll know what not to get.

This is an important lesson for low-sodium living, because if a food has a label, you should be suspicious of it. You don't see a nutritional label on a bunch of broccoli or a fresh fish fillet, but you do see one on every shelf-stable food—including foods that look benign, like a loaf of white bread.

All labels must contain the amount of sodium per serving, and that's why the first place to look on a label is the serving size. If the serving size is 1 teaspoon, and what you would eat as a realistic serving is 3 tablespoons, you'll have to multiply accordingly.

Once you have calculated the serving size, look not only at the number of milligrams of sodium but also at the percentage of the daily value for sodium this represents. But there's the second catch; the daily value is based on 2,400 mg of sodium a day. If you're following a low-sodium diet, which is defined as between 400 mg and 1,000 mg a day, that's more than twice what you should be eating.

Sodium also comes in forms other than table salt, so here are some other words to watch for on labels: baking soda, baking powder, monosodium glutamate (commonly called MSG), sodium alginate, sodium nitrate, or sodium nitrite. Keep an eye on these terms, too.

BEAN COOKERY 101

Beans are justly praised for their nutritional value as well as their availability and economy, and dried beans play a role in almost all the world's cuisines. Beans are a high source of fiber and protein, and they are low in fat and contain no cholesterol. They are also a good source of B vitamins, especially B6.

Until food manufacturers seriously cut back on sodium, canned beans—one of the few "convenience foods" I've used in other *$3 Meals* books—are a thing of the past. You're going to have to cook dried beans, which are virtually sodium-free foods.

I suggest using the slow cooker for this process because you can put the beans in to cook and forget about them, rather than worrying that they're scorching.

Before using beans, rinse them in a colander or sieve under cold running water, and pick through them to discard any broken beans or pebbles that might have found their way into the bag. Then there's a secondary step once the beans have been covered with water; discard any that float to the top.

Then, with the exception of quick-cooking split peas and lentils, dried beans need to be soaked in one of two ways. You can either soak the beans for a minimum of six hours, or up to 12 hours, covered with cold water; that's the slow soak method. Or you can place beans into a saucepan and bring to a boil over high heat. Boil the beans for 1 minute, then turn off the heat, cover the pan, and soak the beans for 1 hour. With either soaking method, drain the beans, discard the soaking water, and begin cooking them as soon as possible. If you can't cook them immediately, then refrigerate them. Once beans are soaked, bacteria can begin to grow.

Cooking beans is common sense: The larger the bean, the longer it will take to soften. But it's not necessary to presoak larger beans for a longer period of time than smaller beans. There's only so much softening that goes on at no or low heat.

Dried beans should be cooked until they are no longer crunchy, but still have texture. If beans are going to be precooked and then cooked further in a dish, such as in a chili, then stop the initial cooking when they are still slightly crunchy. The other caveat of bean cookery is to make sure beans are cooked to the proper consistency before adding any acidic ingredient—such as tomatoes, vinegar, or lemon—because acid prevents the beans from becoming tender. Other factors also enter into the picture. If beans are a few years old, they'll take longer to cook. Also, the minerals in your tap water can retard the softening and require a longer cooking time.

Feel free to flavor beans, as long as salt isn't among the flavorings. I routinely add a few peeled garlic cloves, a bay leaf, some parsley sprigs, halved chile peppers for Hispanic dishes, some slices of ginger (which native Hawaiian cooks say reduces beans' propensity for producing gas), or a chopped onion to the water in which I'm cooking beans.

You can use your slow cooker any time you want to cook beans. Place them in the slow cooker, and cover them with hot water by at least three inches. Keep in mind that beans should be covered with liquid at all times while they're cooking, so toward the end of the cooking process take a look and add boiling water if the water seems almost evaporated.

It makes sense to cook a few pounds of beans at a time, and then freeze them in 1- or 2-cup measures. While you won't have the convenience of canned beans, frozen beans thawed quickly in the microwave are a close second.

Slow Cooker Bean Times

Here's a chart to tell you how long different species of beans should cook in the slow cooker. The calculations in this chart are based on 2 cups of dried beans, which yields 6 cups of cooked beans:

Bean	Cooking Time on High
Black beans	3 hours
Black-eyed peas	$3\frac{1}{4}$ hours
Fava beans	$2\frac{3}{4}$ hours
Garbanzo beans	$3\frac{1}{2}$ hours
Great Northern beans	$2\frac{3}{4}$ hours
Kidney beans	3 hours
Lentils	2 hours (no presoaking)
Lima beans	$2\frac{1}{2}$ hours for baby, $3\frac{1}{2}$ for large
Navy beans	$2\frac{1}{2}$ hours
Split peas	$2\frac{1}{2}$ hours (no presoaking)
White beans	3 hours

Bean Substitution Chart

Bean recipes are very tolerant to substitutions, and the chart on cooking times is a good guide to which one can become a stand-in for another. But color, texture, and flavor are also criteria to consider. Use this chart for guidance.

Bean	What to Substitute
Black (also called turtle)	Kidney
Black-eyed peas	Kidney
Cannellini	Navy
Cranberry	Kidney
Fava (broad beans)	Large Lima
Flageolet	Navy
Kidney (pink and red, pinto)	Navy
Lentils (red, brown, green)	Split peas
Split peas	Lentils

STOCKING UP

Making homemade salt-free stocks is like keeping a cache of cooked beans around; once you've gotten into the habit, it becomes second nature.

Just think about all those parsley stalks, carrot and onion peelings, and celery leaves that end up in the garbage can after you've cooked dinner. And now that you are saving money by cutting up your own chickens (see Chapter 7) or breaking down a large chuck roast into stew cubes (see Chapter 8) all of those scraps and bones become valuable assets, too.

Here's how I navigate the process of stock-making: I keep a few heavy resealable gallon bags in my freezer. Into one go all appropriate vegetable and herb trimmings. Three others are designated for poultry, beef, and fish or seafood trimmings. When one protein bag gets full, I add it to the contents of the vegetable bag, and it's time to make stock.

Once you've made the stock, the next step is to freeze it in convenient forms. Use a measuring tablespoon and calculate the capacity of your ice cube trays; if you have an automatic ice cube maker, then it's worth the few cents to buy a plastic tray too. Freeze some of your stock in the ice cube tray; that's for the times you see "$1/4$ cup chicken stock" in a recipe. Then freeze the remainder in 1-quart plastic bags. Plastic bags take up less room in the freezer than plastic containers. You can freeze the bags flat on a baking sheet and then stack them.

Chicken Stock

Richly flavored homemade chicken stock is as important as good olive oil in my kitchen. Once you've gotten into the habit of "keeping stocked," you'll appreciate the difference that it makes in all soups and sauces. And making it is as easy as boiling water.

Yield: 4 quarts | **Active time:** 10 minutes | **Start to finish:** 4 hours

> 6 quarts water
> 5 pounds chicken bones, skin, and trimmings
> 4 celery ribs, rinsed and cut into thick slices
> 2 onions, trimmed and quartered
> 2 carrots, trimmed, scrubbed, and cut into thick slices
> 2 tablespoons whole black peppercorns
> 6 garlic cloves, peeled
> 4 sprigs parsley
> 2 teaspoons dried thyme
> 2 bay leaves

1. Place water and chicken in a large stockpot, and bring to a boil over high heat. Reduce the heat to low, and skim off foam that rises during the first 10–15 minutes of simmering. Simmer stock, uncovered, for 1 hour, then add celery, onions, carrots, peppercorns, garlic, parsley, thyme, and bay leaves. Simmer for 2½ hours.

2. Strain stock through a fine-meshed sieve, pushing with the back of a spoon to extract as much liquid as possible. Discard solids, spoon stock into smaller containers, and refrigerate. Remove and discard fat from surface of stock, then transfer stock to a variety of container sizes.

Note: The stock can be refrigerated and used within 3 days, or it can be frozen for up to 6 months.

Each ½-cup serving contains:

12 MG SODIUM | 6 calories | 0 calories from fat | 0 g fat | 0 g saturated fat | 0 g protein | 1 g carbohydrates

Variation:
- Substitute turkey giblets and necks for the chicken pieces.

Beef Stock

While beef stock is not specified as often as chicken stock in recipes, it is the backbone to certain soups and the gravy for stews and roasts.

Yield: 2 quarts | **Active time:** 15 minutes | **Start to finish:** 3½ hours

> 2 pounds beef trimmings (bones, fat) or inexpensive beef shank
>
> 3 quarts water
>
> 1 carrot, trimmed, scrubbed, and cut into thick slices
>
> 1 medium onion, peeled and sliced
>
> 1 celery rib, trimmed and sliced
>
> 1 tablespoon whole black peppercorns
>
> 3 sprigs fresh parsley
>
> 1 teaspoon dried thyme
>
> 2 garlic cloves, peeled
>
> 2 bay leaves

1. Preheat the oven broiler, and line a broiler pan with heavy-duty aluminum foil. Broil beef for 3 minutes per side, or until browned. Transfer beef to a large stockpot, and add water. Bring to a boil over high heat. Reduce the heat to low, and skim off foam that rises during the first 10–15 minutes of simmering. Simmer for 1 hour, uncovered, then add carrot, onion, celery, peppercorns, parsley, thyme, garlic, and bay leaves. Simmer for 3 hours.
2. Strain stock through a fine-meshed sieve, pushing with the back of a spoon to extract as much liquid as possible. Discard solids, and spoon stock into smaller containers. Refrigerate; remove and discard fat from surface of stock.

Note: The stock can be refrigerated and used within 3 days, or it can be frozen for up to 6 months.

Each ½-cup serving contains:

15 MG SODIUM | 11 calories | 2 calories from fat | 0 g fat | 0 g saturated fat | 1 g protein | 2 g carbohydrates

Vegetable Stock

You may think it's not necessary to use vegetable stock if making a vegetarian dish that includes the same vegetables, but that's not the case. Using stock creates a much more richly flavored dish that can't be replicated by increasing the quantity of vegetables cooked in it.

Yield: 2 quarts | **Active time:** 10 minutes | **Start to finish:** 1 hour

 2½ quarts water
 2 carrots, scrubbed, trimmed, and thinly sliced
 2 celery ribs, trimmed and sliced
 1 large onion, peeled and thinly sliced
 1 tablespoon whole black peppercorns
 3 sprigs fresh parsley
 2 teaspoons dried thyme
 4 garlic cloves, peeled
 2 bay leaves

1. Pour water into a stockpot, and add carrots, celery, onion, peppercorns, parsley, thyme, garlic, and bay leaves. Bring to a boil over high heat, then reduce the heat to low and simmer stock, uncovered, for 1 hour.
2. Strain stock through a fine-meshed sieve, pushing with the back of a spoon to extract as much liquid as possible. Discard solids, and allow stock to cool to room temperature. Spoon stock into smaller containers, and refrigerate.

Note: The stock can be refrigerated and used within 3 days, or it can be frozen for up to 6 months.

Each ½-cup serving contains:

14 MG SODIUM | 8 calories | 0 calories from fat | 0 g fat | 0 g saturated fat | 0 g protein | 2 g carbohydrates

Seafood Stock

Seafood stock is a great reason to make friends with head of the fish department of your supermarket or a fishmonger, if you're lucky enough to live near a store devoted to fish and seafood. You can arrange in advance to have them save you bodies if the store cooks lobster meat or shells if the store cooks shrimp from scratch, or purchase them at minimal cost.

Yield: 2 quarts | **Active time:** 15 minutes | **Start to finish:** 1¾ hours

> Shells from 3 pounds raw shrimp, or 2 pounds bones and skin from firm-fleshed white fish such as halibut, cod, or sole
>
> 3 quarts water
>
> 1 cup dry white wine
>
> 1 carrot, scrubbed, trimmed, and cut into 1-inch chunks
>
> 1 medium onion, peeled and sliced
>
> 1 celery rib, rinsed, trimmed, and sliced
>
> 1 tablespoon whole black peppercorns
>
> 5 sprigs fresh parsley
>
> 2 teaspoons dried thyme
>
> 3 garlic cloves, peeled
>
> 2 bay leaves

1. If using lobster shells, pull top shell off 1 lobster body. Scrape off and discard feathery gills, then break body into small pieces. Place pieces into the stockpot, and repeat with remaining lobster bodies. If using shrimp shells or fish bones, rinse and place in the stockpot.
2. Add water, wine, carrot, onion, celery, peppercorns, parsley, thyme, garlic, and bay leaves. Bring to a boil over high heat, then reduce the heat to low and simmer stock, uncovered, for 1½ hours.
3. Strain stock through a fine-meshed sieve, pushing with the back of a spoon to extract as much liquid as possible. Discard solids, and allow stock to cool to room temperature. Spoon stock into smaller containers, and refrigerate.

Note: The stock can be refrigerated and used within 3 days, or it can be frozen for up to 6 months.

Each ½-cup serving contains:

10.5 MG SODIUM | 18 calories | 0 calories from fat | 0 g fat | 0 g saturated fat | 0 g protein | 2 g carbohydrates

YEASTY MATTERS

Many cooks are afraid of working with yeast so they do not consider making yeast-risen breads. But the whole process could not be easier, and this section provides a primer on how to work with this live leavening agent that is virtually sodium-free.

All bread depends on the interaction of some sort of flour, liquid, and leavening agent. Wheat flour contains many substances, including protein, starch, lipids, sugars, and enzymes. When the proteins combine with water, they form gluten. Gluten is both plastic and elastic. This quality means that it will hold the carbon dioxide produced by the yeast, but will not allow it to escape or break. It is this plasticity that allows bread to rise before it is baked, at which time the structure of the dough solidifies from the heat.

There are two types of yeast—dry (or granulated) yeast and fresh (or compressed) yeast. Yeast is an organic leavening agent, which means that it must be "alive" in order to be effective. The yeast can be killed by overly high temperatures and, conversely, cold temperatures can inhibit the yeast's action. That is why dry yeast should be refrigerated. It will keep for several months, while fresh yeast is quite perishable and can be held under refrigeration for only 7 to 10 days. The fast-rising yeasts are all dry, and they do cut back on the time needed for rising.

To make sure your yeast is alive, you should start with a step called "proofing." Combine the yeast with warm liquid (110–115°F) and a small amount of flour or sugar. If the water is any hotter, it might kill the yeast. Either use a meat thermometer to take the temperature, or make sure it feels warm but not hot on the underside of your wrist.

Let the mixture rest at room temperature until a thick surface foam forms, which indicates that the yeast is alive and can be used. If there is no foam, the yeast is dead and should be discarded. After your proofing is successful, you are ready to make the dough.

Basic French Bread

This easy recipe is foolproof; I've been making it for years.

Yield: 8 servings | **Active time:** 20 minutes | **Start to finish:** 3 hours

  1 (¼-ounce) package active dry yeast
  1¼ cups warm water (110–115°F)
  1 teaspoon granulated sugar
  3 cups bread flour
  3 tablespoons cornmeal

1. Combine yeast, water, sugar, and ¼ cup flour in a mixing bowl, and whisk well to dissolve yeast. Set aside for 5 minutes, or until mixture begins to become foamy.
2. Transfer mixture to the bowl of a standard electric mixer fitted with the paddle attachment. Add remaining flour, and beat at low speed until flour is incorporated to form a soft dough.
3. Place the dough hook on the mixer, and knead dough at medium speed for 2 minutes. Raise the speed to high, and knead for an additional 3–4 minutes, or until dough is springy and elastic. If kneading by hand, it will take about 10–12 minutes. Oil a mixing bowl and add dough, turning it to make sure top is oiled. Cover bowl with a sheet of plastic wrap, and place it in a warm spot for 1–2 hours, or until dough is doubled in bulk.
4. Lightly oil a baking sheet and sprinkle the center with cornmeal. Punch down dough, and transfer it to a floured surface. Roll or pat dough into a 12 x 6-inch rectangle. Roll dough up tightly from the 12-inch side; shape dough so that ends come to a point. Transfer dough to prepared baking sheet, placing seam down. Cover dough with plastic wrap, and let rise until doubled in bulk, about 45–60 minutes.
5. Preheat the oven to 425°F, and place a low metal pan on the bottom of the oven as it preheats.
6. Slash top of bread in 3 places with a sharp knife. Add ¾ cup water to the hot pan in the oven. Bake bread for 20–30 minutes, or until golden brown and sounds hollow when tapped.
7. Remove the pan from the oven, and cool bread on a rack.

Note: The recipe can be doubled.

Each serving contains:

4 MG SODIUM | 200 calories | 9 calories from fat | 1 g fat | 0 g saturated fat | 7 g protein | 40 g carbohydrates

Basic Focaccia

Italian focaccia, pronounced *foe-KAH-cha,* is one of the world's great nibble foods, as well as being flat so it's perfect for splitting into a sandwich. This low-sodium recipe makes a large pan, and for far less money than boutique bakeries charge for a small section.

Yield: 12 servings | **Active time:** 20 minutes | **Start to finish:** 3½ hours

>3 (¼-ounce) packages active dry yeast
>2¼ cups warm water (110–115°F)
>1 tablespoon granulated sugar
>7 cups all-purpose flour, plus additional if necessary, divided
>½ cup olive oil, divided
>Freshly ground black for sprinkling

1. Combine yeast, water, sugar, and ¼ cup flour in a mixing bowl, and whisk well to dissolve yeast. Set aside for 5 minutes, or until mixture begins to become foamy.
2. Transfer mixture to the bowl of a standard electric mixer fitted with the paddle attachment. Add ⅓ cup oil and remaining flour, and beat at low speed until flour is incorporated to form a soft dough.
3. Place the dough hook on the mixer, and knead dough at medium speed for 2 minutes. Raise the speed to high, and knead for an additional 3–4 minutes, or until dough forms a soft ball and is springy. If kneading by hand, it will take about 10–12 minutes. Oil a mixing bowl, and add dough, turning it to make sure top is oiled. Cover bowl with a sheet of plastic wrap, and place it in a warm spot for 1–2 hours, or until dough is doubled in bulk.
4. Preheat the oven to 450°F, and oil an 11 x 17-inch baking sheet. Gently press dough into the prepared pan; allow dough to rest 5 minutes if difficult to work with. Cover the pan with a sheet of oiled plastic wrap, and let rise in a warm place until doubled in bulk, about 30 minutes.
5. Make indentations in dough at 1-inch intervals with oiled fingertips. Drizzle with remaining oil, and sprinkle with pepper. Bake in lower third of oven until deep golden on top and pale golden on bottom, 25–30 minutes. Transfer bread to a rack and serve warm or at room temperature.

Note: This amount of dough is about the maximum that a standard home mixer can make, so the recipe cannot be increased. However, it can be made smaller proportionally.

Each serving contains:

4 MG SODIUM | 354 calories | 88 calories from fat | 10 g fat | 1 g saturated fat | 8 g protein | 57 g carbohydrates

Variations:

- Sprinkle the top with ¼ cup of a chopped fresh herb such as rosemary, basil, or oregano, or some combination.
- Spread sautéed onions or fennel across the top of the dough before baking.
- Soak 4 garlic cloves, peeled and minced, in the olive oil for 2 hours before making the dough. Either strain and discard garlic, or use it if you really like things garlicky.

The right temperature is necessary for dough to rise. There are some tricks to creating a warm enough temperature in a cold kitchen. Set a foil-covered electric heating pad on low, and put the bowl of dough on the foil; put the bowl in the dishwasher and set it for just the drying cycle; put the bowl in your gas oven to benefit from the warmth of the pilot light; or put the bowl in any cold oven over a large pan of boiling-hot water.

No-Knead White Bread

Starting in about 2007, many cookbook authors and food writers began breaking through the hesitancy of making yeast bread by formulating recipes that would succeed *without* the elbow grease necessary for proper kneading. I played around with a number of these; some were much more successful than others. Here's one, based on a recipe by Mark Bittman from the *New York Times* that I like a lot.

Yield: 12 servings | **Active time:** 10 minutes | **Start to finish:** 5½ hours

1 packet (¼ ounce) instant yeast
1½ cups warm water (110–115°F)
2 teaspoons granulated sugar
3 cups bread flour, divided

1. Combine yeast, water, sugar, and ¼ cup flour in a mixing bowl, and whisk well to dissolve yeast. Set aside for 5 minutes, or until mixture begins to become foamy.
2. Add remaining flour, and stir well; the dough will be loose and shaggy. Cover the bowl loosely with plastic wrap. Set bowl in a warm location, and allow dough to rise for 4 hours.
3. Scrape dough out of the mixing bowl, and place it on a well-oiled surface. Using oiled hands, form the dough into a ball, and cover it loosely with plastic wrap. Allow dough to rest for 30 minutes.
4. Preheat the oven to 450°F, and place a 4–6-quart roasting pan in the oven as it preheats. Carefully place dough ball into the hot pan, cover the pan with its lid or a sheet of aluminum foil, and bake bread for 30 minutes. Uncover the pan, and bake for an additional 20–30 minutes, or until bread is brown and sounds hollow when tapped.
5. Remove the pan from the oven, and cool bread on a rack.

Note: This recipe can be doubled successfully.

Each serving contains:

2 MG SODIUM | 128 calories | 5 calories from fat | 1 g fat | 0 g saturated fat | 4 g protein | 26 g carbohydrates

Variations:
- Add 2 tablespoons of a chopped herb, such as rosemary, oregano, or dill.
- Add ½ cup caramelized diced onion.

USING WOOD CHIPS FOR FLAVOR

If you miss the smoky flavors of bacon or ham, you can still enjoy them without adding sodium to your diet. Wood chips made from aromatic woods like hickory, mesquite, and cherry add immeasurably to the flavor of grilled foods, as well as giving the skin of poultry a rich mahogany color. While Americans use wood chips, grillers around the world have other flavorful additions, such as woody herb sprigs like rosemary or grape vines. In addition you can gain flavor from garlic cloves and pieces of citrus peel.

For charcoal grills the secret is to soak the chips in water to cover for at least 30 minutes. When the coals just begin to form white ash, but are still somewhat red, drain the chips and scatter them over the charcoal.

Even though it won't create as pronounced a flavor, you can also use wood chips on a gas grill. Use about 2 cups dry wood chips. Place them in the center of a large (12 x 18-inch) piece of heavy-duty aluminum foil. Bring up the foil on all sides and roll the ends together to seal the pouch. Poke several small holes in the top of the packet. Once the grill is hot, place the wood chip pouch under the grate across the burner shields. Smoke will eventually emerge from the holes.

BANISHING BLAND

There are certain foods that really need some help to give them flavor when you're on a low-sodium diet, especially inherently delicate foods like pasta, egg noodles, and rice. Without salt, they taste downright bland.

For rice and grains, cooking them with herbs, garlic, and/or chile peppers in stock rather than water solves the problem nicely. Such foods as brown rice, bulgur, buckwheat groats (also called kasha), and wheat berries have an innate nuttiness that compensates well for the lack of salt. Small pasta shapes such as couscous and orzo should be cooked in the same manner.

Pasta and noodles are another matter, however. No one has enough stock around to boil them, nor would it make much difference. The flavoring of these foods comes after they're boiled in water sans salt.

Toss pasta with a bit of olive oil, and then some fresh herbs if you're going to eat it without a sauce. Or cook some herbs and garlic in olive oil, and keep it around as a toss for pasta. For egg noodles, try a few teaspoons of butter; butter goes better with the egg flavor than oil. Then use herbs or poppy seeds to flavor them further.

Chapter 3:
Building Blocks

Condiments and sauces are outrageously expensive, and it's almost impossible to find low-sodium versions. I devoted a chapter in the original *$3 Meals* book to these genres of food because I was outraged at how much they cost relative to the cost of the ingredients. I'm including this chapter in *$3 Low-Sodium Meals* for that reason, too.

This chapter is about your quality of life when adhering to a low-sodium diet. As I said in the introduction to this book, it's possible to tantalize your taste buds while shaking off the shaker. And that means for every aspect of your meal.

The recipes in this chapter are not for whole dishes; those are in the chapters that follow. But these recipes make your food more flavorful and can be utilized in myriad ways. Once you've made a batch of Low-Sodium Marinara Sauce, you can use it to make a quick pasta dish or top a meatloaf. Rather than just using oil and vinegar to flavor a salad, you can enjoy some real dressings that conform to the strict nutritional profile set forth for all recipes in this book, and enjoy that salad more.

Most purchased marinades and mixed spice blends are loaded with sodium, but these ways of adding interest to foods are so quick and easy to make that you'll want to keep them around always.

FLAVORING FOODS WITHOUT FUSS

There are three basic ways to flavor food in a low-sodium way prior to grilling or broiling, and the amount of time each takes to impart taste ranges from a few seconds to coat protein with a spice and herb rub to a few hours to soak food in a marinade.

Rubs are a relative newcomer to the world of flavoring, and while they sit on the surface of foods, they are highly concentrated and bold so that the flavors emerge. While I normally never cook with garlic powder or onion powder, those are necessary in a dry rub to represent those all-important flavors. The best way to handle rubs is to coat the food with olive oil or vegetable oil, and then apply the rub; the oil helps it to adhere.

The middle ground is a paste made with some dry and some wet ingredients; the flavoring should be allowed to penetrate the food for about 15 minutes before cooking.

Marinades all contain some sort of acid, which has the dual benefits of both tenderizing food by breaking down the fibers and perking the palate in the same way that salt does. How much time food needs to marinate depends on what you're making; fish is flavored in as little as 30 minutes, while a steak or chicken piece with skin and bones can soak for up to six hours. Marinades do not work well on vegetables because either the vegetable is too hard to absorb the flavors, as it true with bell peppers or potatoes, or the vegetable absorbs too much marinade to cook well, as is the case with mushrooms and eggplant slices.

As with all recipes in *$3 Low-Sodium Meals,* the marinade recipes have undergone nutritional analysis. But those values should not be taken as dictum; less than 25 percent of a marinade is actually absorbed by the food and the remainder is discarded. So if you're following a low-calorie as well as low-sodium diet, you're actually only gaining a fourth of the calories listed.

LIQUID ASSETS

Vinaigrette dressings—the type used most often—are called temporary emulsions; they will stay blended for only a short time and as the dressing is allowed to stand, the oil and vinegar will gradually separate.

Traditionally, vinaigrettes were made by laboriously whisking the oil into the vinegar. This makes no sense since it will separate in a few moments anyway. That's why for these recipes you are instructed to combine all ingredients in a jar with a tight-fitting lid, and shake well.

This is done in two stages, however. The first is to combine the acid—be it any form of vinegar or citrus juice—with the flavorings and seasonings. Granular substances such as sugar dissolve in water but not in oil, so you want to combine all of those, and then add the oil.

I've often wondered why bottled dressings should be refrigerated after opening; they contain so many preservatives one would think they could survive anything. But your delicious and nutritious homemade dressings should definitely be refrigerated; then allow them to stand at room temperature for 1 hour before serving. Any dressing that contains a dairy product such as sour cream or yogurt, or an egg yolk, should be kept refrigerated until ready to serve.

While many of these recipes were developed for a classic clear vinaigrette, if you want a "creamier" mix, substitute Low-Sodium Mayonnaise (recipe on page 39) for some or all of the oil.

Low-Sodium Mayonnaise

Making mayonnaise in a blender is incredibly easy, and then you can use it any time you want mayonnaise—for salad dressings, to smear on sandwiches, or for any other use.

Yield: 2 cups | **Active time:** 15 minutes | **Start to finish:** 15 minutes

    1 large egg, at room temperature
    2 large egg yolks, at room temperature
    1/2 teaspoon mustard powder
    2 tablespoons lemon juice or more to taste
    2 cups olive oil
    Freshly ground black pepper to taste

1. Combine egg, egg yolks, mustard, and lemon juice in a blender. Blend at high speed for 45 seconds.
2. With the motor running, remove the stopper from the top of the blender, and begin to add oil 1 teaspoon at a time until 1/2 of oil is added and sauce is very thick. Scrape down the sides of the blender beaker.
3. Add remaining oil in 1-tablespoon portions, beating well between each addition. Season to taste with pepper, and add more lemon juice, if desired.

Note: The mayonnaise can be made up to 5 days in advance and refrigerated, tightly covered.

Each 1-tablespoon serving contains:

3 MG SODIUM | 125 calories | 125 calories from fat | 14 g fat | 2 g saturated fat | 1 g protein | 0 g carbohydrates

Variations:
- Add 2–5 peeled garlic cloves for an aioli sauce.
- Add 1–2 tablespoons herbes de Provence or Italian seasoning.
- Add up to 1 teaspoon additional mustard powder.

I've specified using a blender rather than a food processor because you really need the power of the blender and the shape of its narrow beaker to create mayonnaise successfully.

Marvelous Mustard

Like most prepared foods, prepared mustard contains a lot of sodium, although the exact amount depends on the brand. However, mustard powder contains almost no sodium, so you can make your own Dijon-style mustard, and personalize it in myriad ways.

Yield: ½ cup | **Active time:** 10 minutes | **Start to finish:** 10 minutes

½ cup mustard powder
¼ cup boiling water
2 tablespoons white wine vinegar
2 tablespoons white wine
2 teaspoons honey
Freshly ground black pepper to taste

Combine mustard powder, water, vinegar, wine, and honey in a small mixing bowl, and whisk until smooth. Season to taste with pepper.

Note: The mustard can be prepared up to 1 week in advance and refrigerated, tightly covered.

Each 1-tablespoon serving contains:

0.5 MG SODIUM | 10 calories | 0 calories from fat | 0 g fat | 0 g saturated fat | 0 g protein | 2 g carbohydrates

Variations:
- Add 1 tablespoon dried tarragon.
- Increase the honey to 3 tablespoons.
- Add 1 teaspoon wasabi powder.
- Substitute beer for the boiling water and wine.
- Add 2 tablespoons chopped fresh dill.

Creole Rub

Paprika, oregano, and thyme are three ingredients common to much of Creole cooking, and they're the primary flavors in this rub, which can be used on meats, poultry, fish, or vegetables.

Yield: 1/2 cup | **Active time:** 5 minutes | **Start to finish:** 5 minutes

- 3 tablespoons paprika
- 2 tablespoons garlic powder
- 1 tablespoon onion powder
- 1 tablespoon dried oregano
- 1 tablespoon dried thyme
- 2 teaspoons freshly ground black pepper
- 1 teaspoon cayenne

Combine paprika, garlic powder, onion powder, oregano, thyme, pepper, and cayenne in a bowl, and mix well.

Note: Store in an airtight container in a cool, dry place for up to 1 month.

Each 1-tablespoon serving contains:

2 MG SODIUM | 15 calories | 3 calories from fat | 0 g fat | 0 g saturated fat | 1 g protein | 3 g carbohydrates

You'll find both granulated garlic and garlic powder in the supermarket, and you want the powder. The granulated garlic is too coarse to use in a rub.

South of the Border Rub

Here's a rub with all the flavors you'd expect from Mexican food. The smoked paprika adds an almost smoked taste to foods, too. Use it on meats, poultry, fish, or vegetables.

Yield: ½ cup | **Active time:** 5 minutes | **Start to finish:** 5 minutes

    2 tablespoons chili powder
    2 tablespoons smoked Spanish paprika
    1 tablespoon ground cumin
    1 tablespoon ground coriander
    1 tablespoon garlic powder
    1 tablespoon dried oregano
    1 teaspoon freshly ground black pepper
    1 teaspoon crushed red pepper flakes

Combine chili powder, paprika, cumin, coriander, garlic powder, oregano, black pepper, and red pepper in a bowl, and mix well.

Note: Store rub in an airtight container in a cool, dry place for up to 1 month.

Each 1-tablespoon serving contains:

1 MG SODIUM | 3 calories | 1 calorie from fat | 0 g fat | 0 g saturated fat | 0 g protein | 1 g carbohydrates

Mixed Herb and Spice Rub

Aromatic seasonings like cumin and coriander are blended with fresh-tasting herbs in this all-purpose mix, which works well on meats, poultry, fish, or vegetables.

Yield: ½ cup | **Active time:** 5 minutes | **Start to finish:** 5 minutes

    2 tablespoons ground coriander
    2 tablespoons dried thyme
    1 tablespoon ground cumin
    1 tablespoon freshly ground black pepper
    1 tablespoon dried oregano
    1 tablespoon dried sage

Combine coriander, thyme, cumin, pepper, oregano, and sage in a bowl, and mix well.

Note: Store in an airtight container in a cool, dry place for up to 1 month.

Each 1-tablespoon serving contains:

0 MG SODIUM | 3 calories | 1 calorie from fat | 0 g fat | 0 g saturated fat | 0 g protein | 1 g carbohydrates

Lemon Herb Paste

All the aromatic oils of citrus fruits are found in the oil of the colored zest, and those oils add a beguiling fragrance as well as flavor to foods coated with this subtle paste. Rub it on poultry, fish, or pork.

Yield: ½ cup | **Active time:** 10 minutes | **Start to finish:** 10 minutes

- 3 tablespoons dried tarragon
- 2 tablespoons dried thyme
- 2 tablespoons grated lemon zest
- 4 garlic cloves, peeled and pressed through a garlic press
- 2 teaspoons freshly ground black pepper
- 3 tablespoons olive oil

Combine tarragon, thyme, lemon zest, garlic, and pepper in a bowl, and mix well. Add oil, and mix into a paste.

Note: Store in an airtight container, refrigerated, for up to 3 days.

Each 1-tablespoon serving contains:

1 MG SODIUM | 49 calories | 46 calories from fat | 5 g fat | 1 g saturated fat | 0 g protein | 1 g carbohydrates

Variation:
- Substitute lime zest for the lemon zest.

There are many ways to glean zest from citrus fruits, and what's important is to make sure you get just the colored zest and not the bitter white pith beneath it. You can use a gizmo called a zester, the smallest holes on a box grater, or a vegetable peeler.

North African Paste

Lemon is a common flavoring in North African cooking, and along with a combination of parsley and aromatic cilantro it's a dynamite paste for meat, poultry, fish, or vegetables.

Yield: 1 cup | **Active time:** 10 minutes | **Start to finish:** 10 minutes

- 1/2 cup chopped fresh parsley
- 1/2 cup chopped fresh cilantro
- 6 garlic cloves, peeled and pushed through a garlic press
- 1 tablespoon ground cumin
- 1 tablespoon paprika
- 1 teaspoon grated lemon zest
- Crushed red pepper flakes to taste
- 1/3 cup olive oil
- 2 tablespoons lemon juice

Combine parsley, cilantro, garlic, cumin, paprika, lemon zest, and red pepper flakes in a bowl, and mix well. Add oil and lemon juice, and mix into a paste.

Note: Store in an airtight container, refrigerated, for up to 3 days.

Each 2-tablespoon serving contains:

3.5 MG SODIUM | 87 calories | 82 calories from fat | 9 g fat | 1 g saturated fat | 0 g protein | 2 g carbohydrates

Margarita Marinade

Tequila is more than what gives a margarita its kick; it's also a great flavor accent in this spicy marinade for poultry and fish.

Yield: 1½ cups | **Active time:** 10 minutes | **Start to finish:** 10 minutes

- ½ cup lime juice
- ⅓ cup tequila
- 2 jalapeño or serrano chiles, seeds and ribs removed, and finely chopped
- 5 garlic cloves, peeled and minced
- 1 tablespoon grated lime zest
- 2 tablespoons smoked Spanish paprika
- Freshly ground black pepper to taste
- ½ cup olive oil

Combine lime juice, tequila, chiles, garlic, lime zest, paprika, and pepper in a heavy resealable plastic bag, and mix well. Add oil, and mix well again.

Note: The marinade can be refrigerated for up to 3 days.

Each ¼-cup serving contains:

1 MG SODIUM | 198 calories | 163 calories from fat | 18 g fat | 2.5 g saturated fat | 0 g protein | 3 g carbohydrates

(Remember that a maximum of 25 percent of a marinade is actually absorbed by the food.)

> Smoked Spanish paprika is relatively new to the American market, and you'll see from the number of times I call for it how much I like it. The peppers are actually smoked after they're dried, so the flavor and aroma are totally natural.

Citrus Marinade

The delicacy of poultry, pork, and fish takes very well to citrus flavors, especially when they're combined, as in this marinade.

Yield: 1½ cups | **Active time:** 10 minutes | **Start to finish:** 10 minutes

- ³/₄ cup orange juice
- 2 tablespoons lime juice
- 2 tablespoons chopped fresh parsley
- 1 tablespoon dried rosemary, crumbled
- 3 garlic cloves, peeled and minced
- 1 tablespoon grated orange zest
- Freshly ground black pepper to taste
- ¼ cup olive oil

Combine orange juice, lime juice, parsley, rosemary, garlic, orange zest, and pepper in a heavy resealable plastic bag, and mix well. Add oil, and mix well again.

Note: The marinade can be refrigerated for up to 3 days.

Each ¼-cup serving contains:

2 MG SODIUM | 98 calories | 82 calories from fat | 9 g fat | 1 g saturated fat | 0 g protein | 4 g carbohydrates

(Remember that a maximum of 25 percent of a marinade is actually absorbed by the food.)

> Rosemary is one of the few dried spices that need to be handled rather than just added to a dish. The needles release their flavor and aroma only when they're crumbled.

Ginger Chile Marinade

Aromatic sesame oil and fresh-tasting ginger are the dominant ingredients in this Asian marinade. Use it to flavor meats, poultry, or fish.

Yield: 1 cup | **Active time:** 10 minutes | **Start to finish:** 10 minutes

 1/2 cup rice vinegar

 2 tablespoons firmly packed light brown sugar

 3 tablespoons grated fresh ginger

 2 tablespoons chopped fresh cilantro

 2 garlic cloves, peeled and minced

 1 jalapeño or serrano chile, seeds and ribs removed, and finely chopped

 Crushed red pepper flakes to taste

 1/4 cup vegetable oil

 1/4 cup Asian sesame oil*

Combine vinegar, sugar, ginger, cilantro, garlic, chile, and red pepper flakes in a heavy resealable plastic bag, and mix well. Add vegetable oil and sesame oil, and mix well again.

Note: The marinade can be refrigerated for up to 3 days.

Each 1/4-cup serving contains:

4.5 MG SODIUM | 297 calories | 249 calories from fat | 28 g fat | 3.5 g saturated fat | 0 g protein | 9 g carbohydrates

(Remember that a maximum of 25 percent of a marinade is actually absorbed by the food.)

*Available in the Asian aisle of most supermarkets and in specialty markets.

Red Wine Marinade

Less expensive cuts of beef such as round steaks, London broil, and skirt steaks can be tenderized as well as flavored by marinating in this combination of acids for up to 8 hours, and then being grilled or broiled.

Yield: 1 cup | **Active time:** 10 minutes | **Start to finish:** 10 minutes

> ²/₃ cup dry red wine
> 2 tablespoons balsamic vinegar
> 2 tablespoons firmly packed dark brown sugar
> 2 tablespoons chopped fresh parsley
> 1 tablespoon dried thyme
> 3 large garlic cloves, peeled and minced
> 2 bay leaves, crumbled
> Freshly ground black pepper to taste
> ¼ cup olive oil

Combine wine, vinegar, brown sugar, parsley, thyme, garlic, bay leaves, and pepper in a heavy resealable plastic bag, and mix well. Add oil, and mix well again. Add food to be marinated, turning the bag to coat food evenly.

Note: The marinade can be refrigerated for up to 3 days.

Each ¼-cup serving contains:

7 MG SODIUM | 193 calories | 122 calories from fat | 13.5 g fat | 2 g saturated fat | 0 g protein | 10.5 g carbohydrates

(Remember that a maximum of 25 percent of a marinade is actually absorbed by the food.)

Variation:

- To make the marinade appropriate for poultry and fish, substitute dry white wine for the red wine.

> I have a great use for the leftover red wine; I drink it. But to preserve most of a bottle for future cooking, here's what to do: Boil it down in a saucepan until it's reduced by half, then freeze it in ice cube trays. When you're making a dish in the future that calls for red wine, just pull out a few cubes.

Balsamic Vinaigrette

In addition to tossed salads, try this as the dressing on cold pasta salads or drizzle it on grilled meat or poultry.

Yield: 1¼ cups | **Active time:** 5 minutes | **Start to finish:** 5 minutes

2 shallots, peeled and finely chopped
3 garlic cloves, peeled and minced
⅓ cup balsamic vinegar
¼ cup orange juice
2 tablespoons Marvelous Mustard (recipe on page 40)
1 tablespoon chopped fresh parsley
2 teaspoons herbes de Provence
Freshly ground black pepper to taste
½ cup olive oil

Combine shallots, garlic, vinegar, orange juice, mustard, parsley, herbes de Provence, and pepper in a jar with a tight-fitting lid, and shake well. Add olive oil, and shake well again.

Note: The dressing can be made up to 3 days in advance and refrigerated, tightly covered. Bring it back to room temperature before using.

Each 2-tablespoon serving contains:

3 MG SODIUM | 114 calories | 97 calories from fat | 11 g fat | 1.5 g saturated fat | 0 g protein | 4 g carbohydrates

---

Vinaigrette dressings also make an excellent marinade for meat, poultry, or seafood. Combine equal parts of dressing and wine in a heavy resealable plastic bag, and add the food to be marinated. Seafood should be marinated for no more than 30 minutes, while poultry can soak for up to 4 hours, and meats up to 6 hours.

Honey-Herb Vinaigrette

Cider vinegar is one of the mildest on the market, and also one of the most affordable. A bit of sharp mustard balanced by sweet honey makes this a delicious dressing.

Yield: 1 cup | **Active time:** 10 minutes | **Start to finish:** 10 minutes

 ⅓ cup cider vinegar
 1 tablespoon Marvelous Mustard (recipe on page 40)
 1 tablespoon honey
 2 tablespoons chopped fresh parsley
 1 tablespoon herbes de Provence
 1 shallot, peeled and finely chopped
 2 garlic cloves, peeled and minced
 Freshly ground black pepper to taste
 ½ cup olive oil

Combine vinegar, mustard, honey, parsley, herbes de Provence, shallot, garlic, and pepper in a jar with a tight-fitting lid, and shake well. Add olive oil, and shake well again.

Note: The dressing can be made up to 3 days in advance and refrigerated, tightly covered. Bring it back to room temperature before using.

Each 2-tablespoon serving contains:

2 MG SODIUM | 133 calories | 122 calories from fat | 13.5 g fat | 2 g saturated fat | 0 g protein | 3 g carbohydrates

Green Goddess Dressing

William Archer's play, *The Green Goddess,* had a run in San Francisco in the 1920s. Its star, George Arliss, was served a salad with this green-hued dressing specially created for him at the Palace Hotel. It's a wonderful dressing for chicken salad as well as a tossed salad.

Yield: 1¼ cups | **Active time:** 10 minutes | **Start to finish:** 10 minutes

1 cup Low-Sodium Mayonnaise (recipe on page 39)
½ cup firmly packed fresh parsley leaves
2 scallions, white parts and 5 inches of green tops, rinsed, trimmed, and sliced
3 tablespoons white wine vinegar
Freshly ground black pepper to taste

Combine mayonnaise, parsley, scallions, vinegar, and pepper in a blender or food processor fitted with the steel blade. Puree until smooth. Scrape mixture into an airtight container, and refrigerate until serving.

Note: The dressing can be made up to 3 days in advance and refrigerated, tightly covered.

Each 2-tablespoon serving contains:

7 MG SODIUM | 204 calories | 201 calories from fat | 22 g fat | 3 g saturated fat | 1 g protein | 1 g carbohydrates

It's important when measuring foods that are fluffy, like fresh herbs or brown sugar, that they are firmly packed down into the measuring cup. It's the only way to get an accurate measure.

Low-Sodium Southern Barbecue Sauce

This is a sauce I developed many years ago, and I swear by it for all my cooking. Even with the inclusion of a fresh lemon and some ginger, this low-sodium sauce is still a fraction of the price of bottled sauce—and it's delicious.

Yield: 4 cups | **Active time:** 10 minutes | **Start to finish:** 40 minutes

    1 (20-ounce) bottle no-salt-added ketchup
    1 cup cider vinegar
    1/2 cup firmly packed dark brown sugar
    1/4 cup vegetable oil
    2 tablespoons mustard powder
    2 teaspoons wasabi powder
    3 garlic cloves, peeled and minced
    1/4 cup sliced fresh ginger
    1 lemon, thinly sliced
    1/2–1 teaspoon crushed red pepper flakes, or to taste

1. Combine ketchup, vinegar, brown sugar, vegetable oil, mustard, wasabi, garlic, ginger, lemon, and crushed red pepper flakes in a heavy 2-quart saucepan, and bring to a boil over medium heat, stirring occasionally.
2. Reduce the heat to low and simmer sauce, uncovered, for 30 minutes, or until thick, stirring occasionally. Strain sauce, pressing with the back of a spoon to extract as much liquid as possible. Ladle the sauce into containers and refrigerate, tightly covered.

Note: The sauce can be made up to 1 week in advance and refrigerated, tightly covered. Bring it back to room temperature before serving. It can also be frozen for up to 3 months.

Each 2-tablespoon serving contains:

2 MG SODIUM | 53 calories | 15 calories from fat | 2 g fat | 0 g saturated fat | 0 g protein | 8 g carbohydrates

> When making a dish like this one, in which the ginger is strained out, don't bother to take the time to peel it. And when you do peel ginger, save the peels to use in stock if you want some Asian flavors.

Low-Sodium Marinara Sauce

This easy-to-make sauce takes the place of purchased marinara sauce in your repertoire, and because it freezes so well you can keep a batch around at all times.

Yield: 2½ cups | **Active time:** 15 minutes | **Start to finish:** 1 hour

¼ cup olive oil
1 medium onion, peeled and finely chopped
4 garlic cloves, peeled and minced
1 carrot, peeled and finely chopped
1 celery rib, rinsed, trimmed, and finely chopped
2 (14.5-ounce) cans no-salt-added crushed tomatoes
½ cup dry red wine
3 tablespoons chopped fresh parsley
1 tablespoon dried oregano
2 teaspoons dried thyme
2 bay leaves
Freshly ground black pepper to taste

1. Heat olive oil in 2-quart saucepan over medium heat. Add onion and garlic and cook, stirring frequently, for 3 minutes, or until onion is translucent.
2. Add carrot, celery, tomatoes, wine, parsley, oregano, thyme, and bay leaves. Bring to a boil, reduce the heat to low, and simmer sauce, uncovered, stirring occasionally, for 40 minutes, or until lightly thickened. Season to taste with pepper.

Note: The sauce can be made up to 3 days in advance and refrigerated, tightly covered. Bring back to a simmer before serving. It can also be frozen for up to 3 months.

Each ¼-cup serving contains:

22 MG SODIUM | 69 calories | 37 calories from fat | 4 g fat | 1 g saturated fat | 2 g protein | 5 g carbohydrates

Variations:
- Substitute white wine for the red wine.
- Substitute 2 tablespoons herbes de Provence for the oregano and thyme.

Low-Sodium Southwestern Tomato Sauce

This sauce is your "utility infielder" whenever you're serving a Mexican or Southwestern dish. Use it on enchiladas, to moisten and flavor tacos, or in place of salsa with chips.

Yield: 2 cups | **Active time:** 15 minutes | **Start to finish:** 30 minutes

> 1 tablespoon olive oil
> 1 small onion, peeled and finely chopped
> 3 garlic cloves, peeled and minced
> 1–2 jalapeño or serrano chiles, seeds and ribs removed, and finely chopped
> 2 tablespoons chili powder
> 2 tablespoons smoked Spanish paprika
> 1 tablespoon ground cumin
> $3/4$ cup Vegetable Stock (recipe on page 28) or Chicken Stock (recipe on page 26)
> 2 (8-ounce) cans no-salt-added tomato sauce
> $1/4$ cup chopped fresh cilantro
> Freshly ground black pepper to taste

1. Heat olive oil in a 2-quart heavy saucepan over medium heat, swirling to coat the pan. Add onion and garlic and cook, stirring frequently, for 3 minutes, or until onion is translucent. Reduce the heat to low, stir in chiles, chili powder, paprika, and cumin, and cook, stirring constantly, for 1 minute.
2. Stir in stock and tomato sauce. Whisk well, bring to a boil, and simmer sauce, uncovered, for 15 minutes, stirring occasionally, or until the sauce is reduced by $1/4$.
3. Stir in cilantro, and season to taste with pepper. Serve hot or at room temperature.

Note: The sauce can be made up to 3 days in advance and refrigerated, tightly covered. Bring back to a simmer before serving. It can also be frozen for up to 3 months.

Each $1/4$-cup serving contains:

32 MG SODIUM | 45 calories | 15 calories from fat | 2 g fat | 0 g saturated fat | 1 g protein | 7 g carbohydrates

Sweet and Sour Sauce

There are not many Asian recipes in this book because traditional Asian condiments like soy sauce, fish sauce, and hoisin sauce are so high in sodium. But I did develop this delicious sweet and sour sauce to use as an Asian dip for cooked foods.

Yield: 1½ cups | **Active time:** 15 minutes | **Start to finish:** 20 minutes

2 tablespoons Asian sesame oil*
4 scallions, white parts and 4 inches of green tops, rinsed, trimmed, and chopped
3 garlic cloves, peeled and minced
2 tablespoons grated fresh ginger
½ cup finely chopped pineapple
½ cup rice vinegar
⅓ cup no-salt-added ketchup
¼ cup firmly packed dark brown sugar
1 tablespoon reduced-sodium soy sauce
1 tablespoon cornstarch
1 tablespoon cold water

1. Heat oil in a small saucepan over medium-high heat. Add scallions, garlic, and ginger, and cook, stirring frequently, for 3 minutes, or until scallions are translucent.

2. Add pineapple, vinegar, ketchup, sugar, and soy sauce to the pan, and stir well. Bring to a boil over medium-high heat, stirring occasionally. Reduce the heat to low, and simmer sauce, uncovered, for 5 minutes.

3. Combine cornstarch and water in a small cup, and stir well. Add mixture to the pan, and cook for 1 minute, or until slightly thickened. Serve sauce at room temperature or chilled.

Note: The sauce can be refrigerated for up to 1 week.

Each 2-tablespoon serving contains:

35 MG SODIUM | 58 calories | 21 calories from fat | 2 g fat | 0 g saturated fat | 0 g protein | 8 g carbohydrates

*Available in the Asian aisle of most supermarkets and in specialty markets.

Variations:
- Substitute mango or papaya for the pineapple.
- Add $1/2$–1 teaspoon crushed red pepper flakes for a spicy sauce.

Cocktail Sauce

The condiment aisle of the supermarket is loaded with high-sodium, high-priced items with limited use, and cocktail sauce fits into that category.

Yield: 1 cup | **Active time:** 10 minutes | **Start to finish:** 10 minutes

$3/4$ cup no-salt-added ketchup

1 tablespoon wasabi powder

3 tablespoons lemon juice

1 tablespoon balsamic vinegar

$1/4$–$3/4$ teaspoon crushed red pepper flakes

Combine ketchup, wasabi powder, lemon juice, vinegar, and red pepper flakes in a mixing bowl. Whisk well. Scrape mixture into an airtight container, and refrigerate for at least 30 minutes to blend flavors.

Note: The sauce can be made up to 5 days in advance and refrigerated, tightly covered.

Each 2-tablespoon serving contains:

0 MG SODIUM | 38 calories | 0 calories from fat | 0 g fat | 0 g saturated fat | 0 g protein | 7 g carbohydrates

> Mix equal portions of this sauce and Low-Sodium Mayonnaise (recipe on page 39) to make a faux Louis Sauce.

Cilantro Honey Mustard Sauce

I use this sauce on any cold meat, and its heady flavor is so much more appealing than just plain mustard. The aromatic sesame oil lends its own fragrance as well as flavor.

Yield: 1 cup | **Active time:** 5 minutes | **Start to finish:** 5 minutes

> ½ cup Marvelous Mustard (recipe on page 40)
> 2 tablespoons Asian sesame oil*
> 3 tablespoons honey
> ¼ cup chopped fresh cilantro
> Freshly ground black pepper to taste

Combine mustard, honey, and sesame oil in a small bowl. Whisk until smooth. Stir in cilantro, and season to taste with pepper. Serve immediately.

Note: The sauce can be made up to 3 days in advance and refrigerated, tightly covered. Allow it to sit at room temperature for 30 minutes before serving.

Each 2-tablespoon serving contains:

1 MG SODIUM | 66 calories | 32 calories from fat | 3.5 g fat | 0.5 g saturated fat | 0 g protein | 8 g carbohydrates

*Available in the Asian aisle of most supermarkets and in specialty markets.

After you measure the sesame oil, use the same spoon for the honey. The sticky stuff will slide right off the spoon.

Tandoori Indian Sauce

Traditional tandoori chicken is marinated in spiced yogurt before grilling or broiling, but you can achieve the same flavor by using this sauce to top chicken, fish, or meat.

Yield: 1½ cups | **Active time:** 15 minutes | **Start to finish:** 15 minutes

    1 tablespoon vegetable oil
    1 small onion, peeled and finely chopped
    4 garlic cloves, peeled and minced
    2 tablespoons paprika
    1 tablespoon curry powder
    2 teaspoons ground cumin
    1 teaspoon ground ginger
    1 cup plain low-fat yogurt
    ¼ cup lemon juice
    Cayenne to taste

1. Heat oil in a small skillet over medium-high heat. Add onion and garlic, and cook, stirring frequently, for 3 minutes, or until onion is translucent. Add paprika, curry powder, cumin, and ginger, and cook for 1 minute, stirring constantly. Scrape mixture into mixing bowl.
2. Add yogurt and lemon juice to mixing bowl, and whisk well. Season to taste with cayenne, and serve at room temperature.

Note: The sauce can be made up to 3 days in advance and refrigerated, tightly covered. Bring it back to room temperature before serving.

Each 2-tablespoon serving contains:

13 MG SODIUM | 41 calories | 13 calories from fat | 1.5 g fat | 0 g saturated fat | 1 g protein | 6.5 g carbohydrates

Apple and Cranberry Chutney

Chutney is a traditional condiment to go with Indian curries and has an eating profile that is a combination of sweet, sour, and spicy. I love this relish with any cold meat—from turkey and chicken to pork.

Yield: 1½ cups | **Active time:** 15 minutes | **Start to finish:** 40 minutes

> 1 cup cider vinegar
> 1 cup granulated sugar
> 1 pound Granny Smith apples, peeled, cored, and cut into ³/₄-inch dice
> ½ cup dried cranberries
> 1 teaspoon ground ginger
> ½ teaspoon ground cloves
> ½–1 teaspoon crushed red pepper flakes

1. Combine vinegar and sugar in a saucepan, and bring to a boil over medium-high heat. Boil syrup for 10–12 minutes, or until slightly thickened.
2. Add apples, dried cranberries, ginger, cloves, and red pepper flakes. Bring to a boil, reduce the heat to medium, and cook, stirring occasionally, for 15–20 minutes, or until apple softens. Cool to room temperature and then refrigerate, tightly covered.

Note: The chutney can be prepared up to 10 days in advance and refrigerated, tightly covered. Allow it to reach room temperature before serving.

Each ¼-cup serving contains:

3 MG SODIUM | 198 calories | 2 calories from fat | 0 g fat | 0 g saturated fat | 0 g protein | 50 g carbohydrates

Variations:

- Substitute raisins or chopped dried apricots for the dried cranberries.
- Substitute ground cinnamon for the ground ginger.

Onion Chutney

This chutney is more savory than fruity, but the caramelized onions mixed with the spices give it a wonderful depth of flavor. Serve it with any hot or cold simple poultry or meat dish.

Yield: 2 cups | **Active time:** 20 minutes | **Start to finish:** 55 minutes

  2 tablespoons unsalted butter
  2 tablespoons olive oil
  3 sweet onions, such as Bermuda or Vidalia, peeled and diced
  1 tablespoon granulated sugar
  $\frac{1}{2}$ cup balsamic vinegar
  $\frac{1}{3}$ cup firmly packed dark brown sugar
  1 Granny Smith apple, peeled, cored, and chopped
  1 tablespoon mustard powder
  $\frac{1}{2}$ teaspoon ground allspice
  $\frac{1}{2}$ teaspoon ground ginger
  $\frac{1}{2}$ teaspoon crushed red pepper flakes

1. Heat butter and oil in a large saucepan over medium-high heat. Add onions, and toss to coat with fat. Cover the pan, reduce the heat to low, and cook onions for 10 minutes. Uncover the pan, sprinkle onions with sugar, and raise the heat to medium-high. Cook onions for 20–25 minutes, stirring frequently, or until browned.
2. Add vinegar, sugar, apple, mustard, allspice, ginger, and red pepper flakes to the skillet. Reduce the heat to low, and cook, stirring occasionally, for 15–20 minutes, or until thickened.
3. Cool to room temperature and then refrigerate, tightly covered.

Note: The chutney can be prepared up to 10 days in advance and refrigerated, tightly covered. Allow it to reach room temperature before serving.

Each $\frac{1}{4}$-cup serving contains:

16 MG SODIUM | 162 calories | 52 calories from fat | 6 g fat | 2 g saturated fat | 1 g protein | 27 g carbohydrates

Variation:

- Substitute 2 tablespoons curry powder for the mustard, allspice, and ginger.

Chapter 4:
In the Beginning . . .

There's more to a dinner than the entrée. In Chapter 3 you gleaned lots of ideas for ways to dress salads and create easy hot and cold sauces to enliven a simple meal. In this chapter you'll get recipes for wonderful low-sodium dips and some small soups to start your meal.

Dips, served with a selection of healthful fresh vegetable crudités or some crispy carbohydrates, are an easy nibble to nosh with a glass of wine or mug of beer (neither of which is a problem on a low-sodium diet!) before dinner. Or you can place a portion of dip on a bed of chopped lettuce, and serve it as a first course.

Cold soups in summer and hot soups in winter are another of my favorite ways to start a meal. All of these soups are made with richly flavored homemade stocks, which are low in sodium, but boost the flavor of the added ingredients.

DIPS AND DIPPERS

A selection of dips is always a stalwart of entertaining, and they can be very elegant. However, purchasing them—and the foods to dip into them—means that they are probably not low in sodium, and they can become expensive, too. You'll find many recipes in this chapter for a wide variety of dips made with healthful, inexpensive beans as well as other vegetables. Dips can also be made in advance—another of their appealing attributes when entertaining.

A basket of vegetables—often called crudité—can be as simple as carrots and celery, but whatever the contents, the key is to arrange it artistically. I line a low basket with plastic wrap and then cover the plastic with lettuce leaves.

Vegetables such as cauliflower, string beans, and broccoli should be blanched before serving. But rather than dirty a pot, it's more efficient to accomplish this in a microwave. Steam the vegetables for 1–2 minutes, then plunge them into ice water to stop the cooking action. Drain, and you're ready to arrange.

While salt-free crackers are always appropriate, it takes very little effort to create more interesting and inexpensive carbohydrates for dipping. Here are some ideas:

- Pita toasts are easy to make. Separate pita breads into their two natural layers and spread each layer with melted unsalted butter. Sprinkle the pieces with pepper and any herbs you like—anything from oregano to chili powder. Then bake the bread at 375°F for 10–15 minutes, or until browned and crisp. Then break into dipping-size pieces.

- Fried wonton skins are excellent with any Asian dip. Heat oil in a saucepan over medium-high heat to a temperature of 375°F, and cut wonton wrappers into quarters. Fry them for 45–55 seconds, or until brown and crisp. Drain them well on paper towels.

Basic Hummus

Hummus, based on garbanzo beans flavored with sesame, lemon, and garlic, is the onion dip of the twenty-first century. It's ubiquitous with myriad flavor variations in the supermarket and loaded with sodium when you buy it there. You can make it for a fraction of the cost with some cooked beans, and control the sodium, too.

Yield: 10 servings | **Active time:** 10 minutes | **Start to finish:** 10 minutes

   1½ cups cooked garbanzo beans
   ⅓ cup well-stirred tahini
   ¼ cup olive oil
   3 cloves garlic, peeled and minced
   ⅓ cup lemon juice, or to taste
   Freshly ground black pepper to taste

1. Combine garbanzo beans, tahini, olive oil, garlic, and lemon juice in a food processor fitted with the steel blade, and puree until smooth. Scrape mixture into a mixing bowl.
2. Season to taste with pepper, and serve immediately.

Note: The dip can be made up to 2 days in advance and refrigerated, tightly covered. Allow it to reach room temperature before serving.

Each ¼-cup serving contains:

2 MG SODIUM | 136 calories | 92 calories from fat | 10 g fat | 1 g saturated fat | 4 g protein | 9 g carbohydrates

Variations:
- Add up to 3 tablespoons extra lemon juice, plus some lemon zest.
- Add a pureed roasted red bell pepper.
- Add up to 3 more garlic cloves, or up to 3 tablespoons roasted garlic.
- Add ½ cup toasted pine nuts as a garnish.
- Add up to 1 teaspoon crushed red pepper flakes.
- Add 2 tablespoons smoked Spanish paprika.

Tuscan White Bean Dip

This is one of my favorite bean dips; it's visually appealing from the flecks of green parsley, and it's heady with garlic too. I also serve this in place of (or in addition to) butter and olive oil on the table with bread.

Yield: 8 servings | **Active time:** 10 minutes | **Start to finish:** 10 minutes

  2 cups cooked white cannellini beans or navy beans
  1/4 cup olive oil
  1/4 cup lemon juice
  4 garlic cloves, peeled
  1 teaspoon dried thyme
  1/4 cup firmly packed fresh parsley leaves
  Freshly ground black pepper to taste

1. Combine beans, olive oil, lemon juice, garlic, and thyme in a food processor fitted with the steel blade or in a blender. Puree until smooth.
2. Add parsley, and chop finely, using on-and-off pulsing. Season to taste with pepper, and chill well before serving.

Note: The dip can be made up to 2 days in advance and refrigerated, tightly covered. Allow it to reach room temperature before serving.

Each 1/4-cup serving contains:

4 MG SODIUM | 127 calories | 62 calories from fat | 7 g fat | 1 g saturated fat | 4.5 g protein | 12.5 g carbohydrates

Variations:

- Add 1–2 finely chopped roasted red bell peppers.
- Substitute fresh basil for the parsley.

Mexican Kidney Bean Dip

Fresh chile and aromatic spices enliven this hearty dip that is a great way to start any Hispanic meal. You can also smear it on tortillas and toast it for nachos.

Yield: 8 servings | **Active time:** 15 minutes | **Start to finish:** 15 minutes

1/4 cup olive oil
1 small onion, peeled and chopped
1 small jalapeño or serrano chile, seeds and ribs removed, and finely chopped
2 garlic cloves, peeled and minced
1 teaspoon ground coriander
1 teaspoon ground cumin
1/2 teaspoon dried oregano
1 3/4 cups cooked red kidney beans
1/4 cup sour cream
3 tablespoons lime juice
Freshly ground black pepper to taste

1. Heat olive oil in a large skillet over medium-high heat. Add onion, chile, and garlic, and cook, stirring frequently, for 3 minutes, or until onion is translucent. Add coriander, cumin, and oregano, and cook for 1 minute, stirring constantly. Scrape mixture into a mixing bowl, and set aside.
2. Combine beans, sour cream, and lime juice in a food processor fitted with the steel blade, and puree until smooth. Scrape mixture into the mixing bowl with vegetables, season to taste with pepper, and stir well. Serve immediately.

Note: The dip can be prepared up to 2 days in advance and refrigerated, tightly covered. Allow it to reach room temperature before serving.

Each 1/4-cup serving contains:

7 MG SODIUM | 101 calories | 44 calories from fat | 5 g fat | 1 g saturated fat | 4 g protein | 11 g carbohydrates

Baba Ghanouj

This Middle Eastern eggplant dip (pronounced *bah-bah ghan-OUJ*) is also flavored with tahini, a sesame paste. Serve it with pita crisps to be authentic, or with any chip or cracker.

Yield: 10 servings | **Active time:** 15 minutes | **Start to finish:** 1 hour

    2 (1-pound) eggplants
    1/3 cup lemon juice
    3 tablespoons red wine vinegar
    5 garlic cloves, peeled and minced
    2/3 cup well-stirred tahini
    1/4 cup Low-Sodium Mayonnaise (recipe on page 39)
    Freshly ground black pepper to taste

1. Preheat the oven to 450°F. Rinse eggplants under cold water, and prick them with a sharp meat fork or the tip of a paring knife. Bake 20 minutes, turn, and bake an additional 20 minutes, or until flesh is very soft when poked with a meat fork.
2. When eggplants are cool enough to handle, slice them in half and scrape out flesh. Add any juices from the baking pan. Puree in a food processor fitted with the steel blade or pass eggplant pulp through a food mill.
3. Scrape puree into a mixing bowl, and stir in lemon juice, vinegar, garlic, tahini, and mayonnaise. Season to taste with pepper, and serve immediately.

Note: The dip can be made up to 2 days in advance and refrigerated, tightly covered. Allow it to reach room temperature before serving.

Each 1/4-cup serving contains:

4 MG SODIUM | 168 calories | 128 calories from fat | 14 g fat | 2 g saturated fat | 4 g protein | 9 g carbohydrates

Summer Tomato Salsa

Jarred salsa is not worth eating, and the good-quality refrigerated salsa found in the produce department is outrageously expensive and loaded with sodium! You can make this salsa as mild or spicy as you want by cutting back or increasing the number of hot chiles, and in addition to using it as a dip, I also use it as a topping for grilled fish and poultry.

Yield: 8 servings | **Active time:** 15 minutes | **Start to finish:** 1¼ hours, including 1 hour for chilling

> 3 large ripe tomatoes, rinsed, cored, seeded, and chopped
> ¼ red onion, peeled and finely chopped
> ½ green bell pepper, seeds and ribs removed, and finely chopped
> 1–2 jalapeño or serrano chiles, seeds and ribs removed, and finely chopped
> 4 garlic cloves, peeled and minced
> 3 tablespoons chopped fresh cilantro
> 1 teaspoon dried oregano
> 3 tablespoons red wine vinegar
> 2 tablespoons olive oil
> Freshly ground black pepper to taste

Combine tomatoes, onion, green pepper, chile pepper, garlic, cilantro, oregano, vinegar, olive oil, and pepper in a mixing bowl. Stir gently, and refrigerate for at least 1 hour to blend the flavors.

Note: The salsa can be prepared up to 1 day in advance and refrigerated, tightly covered.

Each ¼-cup serving contains:

4 MG SODIUM | 45 calories | 32 calories from fat | 3.5 g fat | 0.5 g saturated fat | 1 g protein | 3 g carbohydrates

Guacamole

Like purchased salsa, you are paying a premium for purchased guacamole, and it's usually loaded with sodium and preservatives, too. The cilantro adds a fresh aroma and finish to this creamy Mexican dip.

Yield: 8 servings | **Active time:** 10 minutes | **Start to finish:** 10 minutes

> 4 ripe avocados
> ½ small red onion, peeled and finely diced
> 1–2 jalapeño or serrano chiles, seeds and ribs removed, and finely diced
> ½ cup chopped fresh cilantro
> 1 teaspoon ground cumin
> ¼ cup lime juice
> Freshly ground black pepper to taste

1. Place avocado, red onion, and chile in a medium mixing bowl. Use a table fork to mash mixture together, leaving some avocado in chunks.
2. Add cilantro, cumin, and lime juice, season to taste with pepper, and mix well. Serve immediately.

Note: The dip can be prepared up to 8 hours in advance. Push a piece of plastic wrap directly into the surface, and then refrigerate.

Each ¼-cup serving contains:

7 MG SODIUM | 119 calories | 93 calories from fat | 10 g fat | 1 g saturated fat | 1.5 g protein | 7.5 g carbohydrates

---

An easy and efficient way to remove the flesh from an avocado is to run a rubber spatula under the skin after the pit has been discarded. You can scrape out the flesh efficiently without the fear of tearing the skin, which would need to be picked out of the dip.

Golden Gazpacho

This bright orange soup has almost a sweet and sour flavor profile from the luscious ripe melon and carrots contrasted with the vinegar and scallions. It's a great variation on the Spanish prototype.

Yield: 6 servings | **Active time:** 15 minutes | **Start to finish:** 2¼ hours, including 2 hours to chill

    4 cups diced ripe cantaloupe
    1 large carrot, peeled and sliced
    2 small cucumbers, peeled, seeded, and sliced
    8 scallions, white parts only, rinsed, trimmed, and sliced
    1–2 jalapeño or serrano chiles, seeds and ribs removed, and diced
    2 garlic cloves, peeled and sliced
    ⅔ cup cider vinegar
    1 cup orange juice
    ¼ cup olive oil
    2 tablespoons lemon juice
    Freshly ground black pepper to taste

1. Combine cantaloupe, carrot, cucumbers, scallions, chiles, garlic, vinegar, orange juice, olive oil, and lemon juice in a food processor fitted with the steel blade or in a blender. Puree until smooth; this may have to be done in batches.
2. Season to taste with pepper. Refrigerate until cold, at least 2 hours.

Note: The soup can be made up to 2 days in advance and refrigerated, tightly covered. Stir it well before serving.

Each serving contains:

28.5 MG SODIUM | 157 calories | 82 calories from fat | 9 g fat | 1 g saturated fat | 2 g protein | 17 g carbohydrates

> Selecting melons is never easy because they have such a hard rind. A general rule is to look at the stem end. It should smell sweet and be flat rather than indented. An indentation is a sign that the melon was pulled off the vine before it was ripe, at which time it comes off easily.

Cream of Celery Soup with Tarragon

Tarragon is an elegant herb with a slightly anise, or licorice, flavor. This soup is subtly seasoned, and the rice used for thickening creates a luscious texture.

Yield: 6 servings | **Active time:** 10 minutes | **Start to finish:** 55 minutes

    4 cups (about ⅔ bunch) celery, rinsed, trimmed, and sliced
    3 cups Chicken Stock (recipe on page 26)
    ½ cup white rice
    1 tablespoon dried tarragon
    1 cup half-and-half
    Freshly ground black pepper to taste

1. Combine celery, stock, rice, and tarragon in a 4-quart saucepan. Bring to a boil over high heat, stirring occasionally. Reduce the heat to low, and simmer soup, partially covered, for 30 minutes.

2. Puree soup in a food processor fitted with the steel blade or in a blender. Return soup to the pan and stir in half-and-half. Bring back to a boil, and simmer 2 minutes. Season to taste with pepper, and serve immediately.

Note: The soup can be made up to 2 days in advance and refrigerated, tightly covered. Reheat it over low heat, covered.

Each serving contains:

83 MG SODIUM | 125 calories | 44 calories from fat | 5 g fat | 3 g saturated fat | 3 g protein | 17 g carbohydrates

Variations:

- Substitute sliced raw fennel for the celery to accentuate the flavor of the tarragon.
- Substitute ¼ cup chopped fresh dill for the tarragon.

Greek Lemon Egg Soup

Called *avgolemono* in Greek cooking, this satiny soup is enlivened with lemon juice and thickened with eggs so it has a custardy texture. If you're serving any Mediterranean meal, here's your starter.

Yield: 6 servings | **Active time:** 20 minutes | **Start to finish:** 30 minutes

7 cups Chicken Stock (recipe on page 26)
3/4 cup orzo
4 large eggs
1/2 cup lemon juice
Freshly ground black pepper to taste

1. Bring stock to a boil over medium-high heat. Add orzo and cook, covered, for 9–12 minutes, or until orzo is tender; the length of time depends on the brand of pasta.
2. While stock simmers, whisk eggs well with lemon juice. Remove the pan from the heat, and stir for 45 seconds to cool soup. The liquid should not be bubbling or simmering at all. Stir in egg mixture, cover the pan, and let soup sit for 5 minutes to thicken.
3. Season soup to taste with pepper, and serve immediately.

Note: The soup can be prepared 1 day in advance and refrigerated, tightly covered. Reheat it over very low heat, stirring frequently, and do not allow it to boil or the eggs will scramble.

Each serving contains:

77 MG SODIUM | 146 calories | 33 calories from fat | 4 g fat | 1 g saturated fat | 7.5 g protein | 21 g carbohydrates

Variations:

- Substitute rice for the orzo. Cook rice for 12–15 minutes, or until rice is tender.
- Add 1 (10-ounce) box frozen mixed vegetables along with the orzo.

Austrian Red Cabbage Soup

Red cabbage is the mild cousin in the family, and its inherent sweetness is amplified by hints of heady balsamic vinegar contrasted with brown sugar.

Yield: 6 servings | **Active time:** 20 minutes | **Start to finish:** 1¼ hours

    1 (1½-pound) red cabbage
    2 tablespoons vegetable oil
    1 large red onion, peeled and diced
    2 garlic cloves, peeled and minced
    5 cups Vegetable Stock (recipe on page 28)
    1 (14.5-ounce) can no-salt-added diced tomatoes, undrained
    ¼ cup balsamic vinegar
    ¼ cup firmly packed dark brown sugar
    2 tablespoons chopped fresh parsley
    1 teaspoon dried thyme
    1 bay leaf
    Freshly ground black pepper to taste
    6 tablespoons sour cream (optional)

1. Discard outer leaves from red cabbage. Cut cabbage in half and discard core. Shred cabbage finely, and set aside; this can be done quickly using a food processor fitted with a thin slicing disc.

2. Heat oil in a 3-quart saucepan over medium-high heat. Add onion and garlic, and cook, stirring frequently, for 3 minutes, or until onion is translucent. Add cabbage, stock, tomatoes, balsamic vinegar, brown sugar, parsley, thyme, and bay leaf. Bring to a boil over high heat, stirring occasionally.

3. Reduce the heat to low, and simmer soup, partially covered, for 1 hour, or until cabbage is very tender. Remove and discard bay leaf, season to taste with pepper, and serve hot, garnished with sour cream, if using.

Note: The soup can be made up to 2 days in advance and refrigerated, tightly covered. Reheat it over low heat, covered.

Each serving contains:

87.5 MG SODIUM | 159 calories | 43 calories from fat | 5 g fat | 0.5 g saturated fat | 3 g protein | 28 g carbohydrates

Cuban Black Bean Soup

Garlic and aromatic spices like cumin and coriander add sparkle to this thick and hearty vegetarian soup. Add a tossed salad and some garlic bread, and the meal is complete.

Yield: 6 servings | **Active time:** 15 minutes | **Start to finish:** 2 hours, including 1 hour for soaking beans

> 1 pound dried black beans
> 1/4 cup olive oil
> 1 large onion, peeled and diced
> 1 green bell pepper, seeds and ribs removed, and finely chopped
> 6 garlic cloves, peeled and minced
> 1–2 jalapeño or serrano chiles, seeds and ribs removed, and finely chopped
> 2 tablespoons ground cumin
> 1 tablespoon ground coriander
> 6 cups Vegetable Stock (recipe on page 28)
> 1/4 cup chopped fresh cilantro
> Freshly ground black pepper to taste
> Sour cream (optional)
> Lime wedges (optional)

1. Soak beans in cold water to cover for a minimum of 6 hours, or preferably overnight. Or, place beans in a saucepan covered with water, and bring to a boil over high heat. Boil for 1 minute, turn off the heat, and cover the pan. Allow beans to soak for 1 hour, then drain. With either method, continue with the dish as soon as beans have soaked, or refrigerate beans.

2. Heat oil in a 3-quart saucepan over medium-high heat. Add onion, green bell pepper, garlic, and chiles. Cook, stirring frequently, for 3 minutes, or until onion is translucent. Reduce the heat to low, and stir in cumin and coriander. Cook, stirring constantly, for 1 minute.

3. Add beans and stock, and bring to a boil over high heat, stirring occasionally. Reduce the heat to low, and simmer soup, partially covered, for 1–1¼ hours, or until beans are soft.

4. Remove 2 cups of beans with a slotted spoon, and puree in a food processor fitted with the steel blade or in a blender. Return beans to the soup, stir in cilantro, season to taste with pepper, and serve hot. Top with a dollop of sour cream and serve with lime wedges, if using.

Note: The soup can be made up to 2 days in advance and refrigerated, tightly covered. Reheat it over low heat, covered.

Each serving contains:

22 MG SODIUM | 330 calories | 52 calories from fat | 6 g fat | 1 g saturated fat | 17 g protein | 55 g carbohydrates

There's no question that chiles contain potent oils; however, there's no need to wear rubber gloves when handling them. I cut the chiles on a glass plate rather than on my cutting board so the volatile oils do not penetrate. What's most important is that you wash your hands thoroughly after handling chiles.

Southwestern Vegetable Soup

My travels have served as the basis for many dishes, including this one, inspired by the Sopa Azteca that is part of traditional Southwestern cooking. It is the specialty of El Mirador in San Antonio, Texas. It's spicy, and while it's cooking the kitchen is filled with glorious, promising aromas.

Yield: 6 servings | **Active time:** 20 minutes | **Start to finish:** 40 minutes

1 tablespoon olive oil
1 medium onion, peeled and diced
2 garlic cloves, peeled and minced
1 (14.5-ounce) can no-salt-added tomatoes, drained
2 teaspoons dried oregano
2 teaspoons dried basil
1 teaspoon ground cumin
4 cups Vegetable Stock (recipe on page 28)
3 tablespoons no-salt-added tomato paste
3 celery ribs, rinsed, trimmed, and sliced
1 small green bell pepper, seeds and ribs removed, and diced
2 medium zucchini, rinsed, trimmed, and sliced
1 large carrot, peeled and diced
1 large redskin potato, scrubbed and cut into 1/2-inch dice
1/2 cup cooked kidney beans
Freshly ground black pepper to taste
3 (6-inch) corn tortillas
Vegetable oil spray

1. Heat oil in a 4-quart saucepan over medium-high heat. Add onion and garlic, and cook, stirring frequently, for 3 minutes, or until onion is translucent. Add tomatoes, oregano, basil, and cumin. Cook mixture for 10 minutes over medium heat, stirring frequently.

2. Transfer vegetable mixture to a food processor fitted with the steel blade or to a blender; puree until smooth. Return mixture to the pan, and add stock and tomato paste, stirring well to dissolve tomato paste. Bring to a boil over medium heat.

3. Add celery, green bell pepper, zucchini, carrot, potato, and kidney beans to soup and simmer, uncovered, for 15 minutes, or until the vegetables are cooked through but retain their texture. Season to taste with pepper.

4. While soup simmers, preheat the oven to 375°F. Cut each tortilla into 8–10 triangles, and spray lightly with vegetable oil spray. Arrange tortilla wedges on a baking sheet, and bake for 5 minutes, turning once, or until tortilla wedges are crisp. To serve, ladle soup into shallow bowls, and top each serving with tortilla wedges.

Note: The soup can be made up to 3 days in advance, and refrigerated, tightly covered. Reheat it slowly and don't allow it to simmer, or the vegetables will overcook.

Each serving contains:

72 MG SODIUM | 146 calories | 28 calories from fat | 3 g fat | 0.5 g saturated fat | 5 g protein | 27 g carbohydrates

Variations:

- Substitute chicken stock for the vegetable stock, and add ½ pound boneless, skinless chicken breast, cut into ½-inch cubes, along with the vegetables. Make sure chicken is cooked through and no longer pink.
- Add 1–2 jalapeño or serrano chiles, seeds and ribs removed and sliced, to the onion mixture being cooked for a spicy dish.

Chapter 5:
Vegetarian Versatility

The "occasional vegetarian" is a term applied to many folks in these penny-pinching times. This is a person who has not given up animal protein, but who follows a vegetarian regimen a few times a week for reasons of both economy and health. There's no question that most of us could add more vegetables to our diet, as well as more fruits; this style of eating accomplishes that goal.

The world's cuisines are full of diverse vegetarian recipes, and these are what you will find in this chapter. From Indian lentils to Italian baked pasta, the options for delicious low-sodium meals are a cornucopia of riches.

All low-sodium bean dishes are made with beans that have been rehydrated from dried beans to avoid the sodium used in processing beans found ready to use in cans. For information on how to cook the beans, refer to pages 22 to 24.

COMPLETING PROTEINS

The reason why there are so many dishes that pair beans with rice or pasta is more than flavor. What generations before us knew instinctively, and we now know scientifically, is that the protein in legumes such as beans is "incomplete." This means that in order to deliver their best nutritional content, beans need to be paired with carbohydrate-rich grains such as rice.

When the beans and grains are eaten together, they supply a quality of protein that's as good as that from eggs or beef. There is still some debate as to whether the legumes and carbohydrates have to be eaten literally off the same plate, or within a few hours of each other to gain the beneficial effect.

TERRIFIC TOFU

No wonder they call it a wonder food! Lately, researchers are discovering more and more nutritional benefits of soy products. For example, soybeans are the only known plant source of complete protein, for adults although not for children.

Complete protein is the term used for a food that contains all the essential amino acids in the appropriate proportions that are part of the growth and maintenance of cells. Meats and some dairy products have complete protein, while grains and beans contain incomplete proteins. Blending incomplete proteins such as rice and beans produces complete protein. But in the plant world, soy alone has it all.

In addition, the Food and Drug Administration (FDA) has approved a health claim stating that diets containing 25 grams soy protein a day may reduce the risk of heart disease. This should be good news when you're on a low-sodium diet.

While soy milk is growing in popularity as an alternative to cow's milk, the way we eat soybeans most often is as tofu, a custard-like substance, also called bean curd, which is the literal translation. Tofu's innate flavor is very mild, so it absorbs the flavor of the sauce in which it's cooked.

Making tofu is similar to making cheese. Both methods involve curds and whey. For tofu the first step is to create soy milk by soaking, grinding, boiling, and straining dried soybeans. The milk then has either salts or acids added to cause coagulation. Then the curds are extracted from the whey and packaged. The texture of tofu depends on the amount of water pressed out. Here are the three consistencies in the supermarket:

- **Soft (or silken) tofu.** This tofu has had no water removed, and it has the texture of a silky custard. While it's great added to smoothies or juices, it does not hold together when cooked.

- **Firm tofu.** Some whey has been pressed out, so this tofu has the texture of raw meat, although that texture will not change once it's cooked. It bounces back when pressed with your finger, and it can easily be picked up by chopsticks or a fork.

- **Dry (also called extra-firm) tofu.** The most solid of all tofu, it has the texture of cooked meat and crumbles easily. It's this type of tofu that's used in processed tofu products.

What's confusing when looking at tofu packages is that the net weights vary although the package size is uniform because the net weight is that of the product with the weight of the surrounding water subtracted from the total. Silken tofu packages weigh 1 pound, while the net weight of firm tofu can vary from 12 to 14 ounces, depending on the brand. Dry tofu can have a net weight as low as 8 ounces.

Tofu is a vegetable product, but it is as perishable as delicate seafood; make sure you look for the "sell by" date before buying it. Tofu is packed in water, and the water should be changed daily once it's home and the package has been opened. It will last up to a week with fresh water daily, but may spoil within a few days otherwise. Tofu can be frozen for up to three months. The texture will change to become slightly chewy after it thaws.

You'll notice that these recipes specify light tofu, which is relatively new to the market. It is a reduced calorie product, and I can tell no difference in the flavor or texture. A portion of firm tofu has about 70 calories, while there are only 40 calories in the light version.

QUICHE QUICKIE

Quiche, pronounced *keesh,* originated in the Alsace-Lorraine region of northeastern France. The only common denominators that define a quiche are that the base is an egg and cream custard and it's baked as an open-faced tart. Other than that, it's all up to you.

One step that should not be skipped is partially baking the crust before the filling is added. This ensures a crispy crust. But both the pre-baking of the pie shell and making the filling can be done in advance, and the final baking time is less than 30 minutes. While quiche can be fully baked in advance and reheated, they look so pretty coming to the table puffed right from the oven that it's a shame to miss that visual part of the experience.

Quiche are cooked when the egg mixture no longer jiggles in any way and a knife inserted into the center comes out clean, without any particles of egg clinging to it.

Barbecued Tofu

Slices of tofu are coated with a spice mixture and then fried to give them a crispy exterior and make this a dish that's low-sodium but loaded with flavor. Serve the tofu with steamed vegetables or stewed beans.

Yield: 6 servings | **Active time:** 5 minutes | **Start to finish:** 15 minutes

3 tablespoons chili powder

2 tablespoons smoked Spanish paprika

1 tablespoon ground cumin

2 teaspoons dried oregano

Freshly ground black pepper to taste

$1/2$ cup boiling water

$1/3$ cup pure maple syrup

$1/4$ cup lemon juice

2 (14-ounce) packages light firm tofu

2 tablespoons vegetable oil

1. Combine chili powder, paprika, cumin, oregano, and pepper in a small bowl. Combine boiling water, maple syrup, and lemon juice in a small cup. Drain tofu, pat dry with paper towels, and cut each package into 6 slices. Rub spice mixture on both sides of slices.

2. Heat oil in a large skillet over medium-high heat, swirling to coat the pan. Add tofu, and cook for 4–5 minutes, or until brown and crusty. Turn slices gently with a slotted spatula, and cook the remaining side for 4–5 minutes; this may have to be done in batches. Add maple syrup mixture to the pan, and shake the pan to coat slices. Serve immediately.

Note: The tofu can be prepared for frying up to 1 day in advance and refrigerated, tightly covered.

Each serving contains:

153 MG SODIUM | 143 calories | 54 calories from fat | 6 g fat | 1 g saturated fat | 8 g protein | 15 g carbohydrates

Variation:

- Substitute paprika for the chili powder for a less spicy dish, and substitute 2 teaspoons Italian seasoning for the ground cumin and oregano.

Crunchy Wasabi Tofu

These Asian-spiced patties are almost like burgers. The spicy mayonnaise sauce gives them creaminess, along with some bite.

Yield: 6 servings | **Active time:** 15 minutes | **Start to finish:** 20 minutes

    2 (12–14-ounce) packages light firm tofu
    ½ cup blanched slivered almonds
    ½ cup Low-Sodium Mayonnaise (recipe on page 39)
    1½ teaspoons wasabi paste*
    2 large eggs, lightly beaten
    5 scallions, white parts and 4 inches of green tops, rinsed,
       trimmed, and thinly sliced
    3 garlic cloves, peeled and minced
    1 tablespoon grated fresh ginger
    1 tablespoons reduced-sodium soy sauce
    Freshly ground black pepper to taste
    ½ cup panko breadcrumbs*
    ½ cup sesame seeds*
    3 tablespoons Asian sesame oil *
    2 tablespoons vegetable oil

1. Preheat the oven to 350°F. Drain tofu, cut into 1-inch-thick slices, and wrap in several layers of paper towels. Place a pan on top of tofu, and weight the pan with 5 pounds of food cans. Allow tofu to drain for 5 minutes. Place almonds on a baking sheet, and bake for 5–7 minutes, or until browned. Chop almonds coarsely, and set aside. Combine mayonnaise and wasabi paste in a small bowl, and stir well. Refrigerate until ready to use.

2. Transfer tofu to a medium mixing bowl, and mash into small pieces with a potato masher or a large fork. Add almonds, eggs, scallions, garlic, ginger, and soy sauce to tofu. Season to taste with pepper, and mix well. Form mixture into 6 (½-inch-thick) patties.

3. Combine panko and sesame seeds in a small bowl. Pat mixture on both sides of patties.

*Available in the Asian aisle of most supermarkets and in specialty markets.

4. Heat sesame oil and vegetable oil in a large skillet over medium heat. Add tofu patties, and cook for 3-4 minutes per side, or until browned. Turn patties gently with a slotted spatula, and cook on the other side. Remove patties from the skillet, and drain on paper towels. Serve immediately, passing wasabi mayonnaise separately.

Note: The tofu mixture can be prepared up to 1 day in advance and refrigerated, tightly covered.

Each serving contains:

206 MG SODIUM | 474 calories | 377 calories from fat | 42 g fat | 6 g saturated fat | 14.5 g protein | 12 g carbohydrates

Variation:
- Add $1/2$-1 teaspoon crushed red pepper flakes to the tofu mixture for a spicier dish.

Wasabi, pronounced *wah-sah-bee*, is a Japanese form of horse-radish that's light green and has a sharp, fiery flavor. It's sold both as paste and powder, and the powder is mixed with water like dry mustard to make a paste. In a pinch you can use bottled Western horseradish.

Greek Spinach and Feta Quiche

Feta adds great sharp flavor to this quiche without adding significant sodium, and the aromatic fresh dill is a nice counterpoint.

Yield: 6 servings | **Active time:** 15 minutes | **Start to finish:** 40 minutes

1 Basic Piecrust for 9-inch single pie (recipe on page 228)
1 (10-ounce) package frozen chopped spinach, thawed
2 tablespoons unsalted butter
1 tablespoon olive oil
1/2 green bell pepper, seeds and ribs removed, and finely chopped
4 scallions, white parts and 3 inches of green tops, rinsed, trimmed, and sliced
2 garlic cloves, peeled and minced
3 large eggs
1 1/4 cups half-and-half
1/2 cup crumbled feta cheese
3 tablespoons chopped fresh dill or 1 tablespoon dried
Freshly ground black pepper to taste

1. Preheat the oven to 400°F. Prick pie shell all over with the tines of a fork and bake for 8–9 minutes, or until pastry is set and just starting to brown. Remove crust from the oven, and set aside. Place spinach in a colander, and press with the back of a spoon to extract as much liquid as possible.

2. While crust bakes, heat butter and olive oil in a large skillet over medium-high heat. Add green bell pepper, scallions, and garlic, and cook, stirring frequently, for 3 minutes, or until scallions are translucent. Add spinach, and cook for 1 minute. Cool mixture for 5 minutes.

3. Reduce the oven temperature to 375°F. Whisk eggs with half-and-half, feta, and dill, and season to taste with pepper. Stir in spinach mixture, fill pie shell, and bake quiche for 25–30 minutes, or until browned and eggs are set. Serve immediately, or at room temperature.

Note: The filling can be prepared 1 day in advance and refrigerated, tightly covered. Add 5–7 minutes to the baking time if filling is chilled. The crust can be baked 1 day in advance and kept at room temperature, covered in plastic wrap.

Each serving contains:

97 MG SODIUM | 404 calories | 263 calories from fat | 29 g fat | 16.5 g saturated fat | 10 g protein | 27 g carbohydrates

Variation:
- Substitute frozen chopped broccoli, cooked according to package directions, and drained, for the spinach.

Frozen spinach can be used without cooking it first because the initial blanching of the leaves before freezing is sufficient to cook the vegetable. The spinach will also retain its pretty bright green color.

Provençale Vegetable Quiche

The combination of vegetables in this custard is similar to a classic French ratatouille. The Swiss cheese is a mellow contrast.

Yield: 6 servings | **Active time:** 15 minutes | **Start to finish:** 40 minutes

  1 Basic Piecrust for 9-inch single pie (recipe on page 228)
  3 tablespoons unsalted butter
  1 tablespoon olive oil
  1 medium onion, peeled and chopped
  2 garlic cloves, peeled and minced
  2 small zucchini, rinsed, trimmed, and thinly sliced
  3 large eggs
  1½ cups half-and-half
  2 tablespoons all-purpose flour
  ½ cup grated Swiss cheese
  2 tablespoons chopped fresh parsley
  2 teaspoons herbes de Provence
  Freshly ground black pepper to taste
  2 cups grape tomatoes, rinsed, stemmed if necessary, and patted
    dry with paper towels

1. Preheat the oven to 400°F. Prick pie shell all over with the tines of a fork and bake for 8–9 minutes, or until pastry is set and just starting to brown. Remove crust from the oven, and set aside.
2. Heat butter and oil in a skillet over medium heat. Add onion, garlic, and zucchini, and cook, stirring frequently, for 5–7 minutes, or until vegetables are soft.
3. While vegetables cook, whisk eggs with half-and-half and flour in a mixing bowl. Stir in Swiss cheese, parsley, and herbes de Provence, and season to taste with pepper.
4. Reduce the oven temperature to 375°F. Arrange vegetables and tomatoes in the prepared pan, and pour custard on top. Bake quiche for 25–30 minutes, or until browned and eggs are set. Serve immediately, or at room temperature.

Note: The filling can be prepared 1 day in advance and refrigerated, tightly covered. Add 5–7 minutes to the baking time if filling is chilled. The crust can be baked 1 day in advance and kept at room temperature, covered in plastic wrap.

Each serving contains:

95 MG SODIUM | 489 calories | 314 calories from fat | 35 g fat | 20 g saturated fat | 13 g protein | 33 g carbohydrates

Variation:
- Substitute cheddar cheese for the Swiss cheese.

The reason to add flour to this recipe is that the tomatoes will give off liquid as they cook, and the flour prevents the custard from becoming watery.

Baked Rigatoni with Broccoli Rabe

Broccoli rabe, sometimes sold as rapini in supermarkets, is a more robustly flavored version of standard broccoli. It adds vibrancy to this easy baked pasta dish.

Yield: 6 servings | **Active time:** 20 minutes | **Start to finish:** 50 minutes

2 tablespoons olive oil
1 medium onion, peeled and diced
2 garlic cloves, peeled and minced
$\frac{1}{4}$ cup vodka
1 (8-ounce) can no-salt-added tomato sauce
1 (14.5-ounce) can no-salt-added diced tomatoes, undrained
1 cup half-and-half
2 teaspoons dried oregano
2 teaspoons dried thyme
$\frac{1}{4}$ teaspoon crushed red pepper flakes
1 pound broccoli rabe, tough stems discarded, and cut into 1-inch lengths
$\frac{2}{3}$ pound rigatoni
Freshly ground black pepper to taste
$\frac{1}{4}$ cup freshly grated Parmesan cheese

1. Preheat oven to 375°F, and grease a 9 x 13-inch baking pan.
2. Heat oil in saucepan over medium heat. Add onion and garlic, and cook, stirring frequently, for 3 minutes, or until onion is translucent. Add vodka, and cook until liquid has almost evaporated, about 3 minutes. Stir in tomato sauce, tomatoes, half-and-half, oregano, thyme, and red pepper flakes. Bring to a boil, then reduce the heat to low, and simmer for 15 minutes, stirring occasionally.
3. Bring a large pot of salted water to a boil, and have a bowl of ice water handy. Add broccoli rabe, and blanch for 1 minute. Remove broccoli rabe from pan with a slotted spoon, and plunge into ice water to stop the cooking action. Once chilled, drain and set aside. Add rigatoni to water, and cook according to package directions for 2 minutes less than suggested. Drain, return pasta to pot, and stir in sauce and broccoli rabe. Season to taste with pepper.

4. Transfer mixture to the prepared pan, and cover the pan with aluminum foil. Bake for 10 minutes. Remove foil, and sprinkle with cheese. Return pan to oven for 20 minutes, or until mixture is bubbling and top is slightly browned. Serve immediately.

Note: The dish can be prepared for baking up to 2 days in advance and refrigerated, tightly covered. Add 15 minutes to the covered baking time if chilled.

Each serving contains:

105.5 MG SODIUM | 339 calories | 91 calories from fat | 10 g fat | 4 g saturated fat | 12 g protein | 47.5 g carbohydrates

Variation:
- Substitute regular broccoli or kale for the broccoli rabe.

Blanching is a preliminary cooking given to green vegetables and some fruits. The food is plunged into rapidly boiling water, and then removed and plunged into ice water to stop the cooking process. For vegetables, it sets the color, while for fruits such as peaches and tomatoes, it makes the skins easy to slide off.

Baked Eggs with Garden Vegetables

This is a great dish for a summer brunch as well as a light supper. The eggs are baked in small indentations made in the melange of vegetables.

Yield: 6 servings | **Active time:** 20 minutes | **Start to finish:** 30 minutes

¼ cup olive oil

2 tablespoons unsalted butter

6 scallions, white parts and 3 inches of green tops, rinsed, trimmed, and thinly sliced

1 green bell pepper, seeds and ribs removed, and chopped

½ pound mushrooms, wiped with a damp paper towel, trimmed, and thinly sliced

3 garlic cloves, peeled and minced

6 ripe plum tomatoes, rinsed, cored, seeded, and chopped

2 tablespoons chopped fresh parsley

1 tablespoon herbes de Provence

Freshly ground black pepper to taste

12 large eggs

½ cup grated Swiss cheese

1. Preheat the oven to 350°F, and grease a 9 x 13-inch baking pan.
2. Heat oil and butter in a medium skillet over medium heat. Add scallions, green bell pepper, mushrooms, and garlic. Cook, stirring frequently, for 3 minutes, or until scallions are translucent. Add tomatoes, parsley, and herbes de Provence, raise the heat to medium-high, and cook, stirring frequently, for 5 minutes, or until the mixture has slightly thickened and the liquid has almost evaporated. Season vegetables to taste with pepper.
3. Transfer vegetables to the prepared baking pan, and spread in an even layer. Make 12 depressions in the vegetables with the back of a spoon and break an egg into each. Sprinkle eggs with pepper and then sprinkle cheese over the top of eggs and vegetables.
4. Bake for 12–15 minutes, or until the eggs are just set. Serve immediately.

Note: The vegetable mixture can be prepared 1 day in advance and refrigerated, tightly covered. Reheat it over low heat until hot before adding eggs and baking.

Each serving contains:

173 MG SODIUM | 320 calories | 216 calories from fat | 24 g fat | 8 g saturated fat | 18 g protein | 10 g carbohydrates

Variation:
- Substitute 2 medium zucchini or yellow squash, rinsed, trimmed, and thinly sliced, for the green bell pepper.

When buying mushrooms, it's best to choose loose ones rather than pre-packaged. Look for tightly closed mushrooms. Once the brown gills on the bottom are showing, they are past their prime.

Spicy Sweet Potato Pancakes

I think sweet potatoes are one of the more underutilized vegetables; they add so much flavor as well as glorious color to dishes, and they're usually relegated to holiday meals. These crispy pancakes balance the potatoes' inherent sweetness with fiery chiles, and the crispy exterior adds textural contrast.

Yield: 6 servings | **Active time:** 25 minutes | **Start to finish:** 25 minutes

> 4 large sweet potatoes (about 2½ pounds total), scrubbed and cut into 1-inch dice
> 1 medium onion, peeled and cut into 1-inch dice
> 2 large eggs
> 3 tablespoons all-purpose flour
> ½ cup chopped fresh cilantro
> 2 jalapeño or serrano chiles, seeds and ribs removed, and finely chopped
> 1 tablespoon ground cumin
> Freshly ground black pepper to taste
> ½ cup vegetable oil
> 1 cup sour cream
> 1 cup Summer Tomato Salsa (recipe on page 68)

1. Preheat the oven to 200°F; line a baking sheet with aluminum foil.
2. Place 1 cup sweet potato cubes in the work bowl of a food processor fitted with the steel blade. Chop finely using on-and-off pulsing. Scrape potatoes into a colander, and repeat until all sweet potatoes and onion are finely chopped. (You can also do this through the large holes of a box grater.) Press on sweet potatoes and onion with the back of a spoon to extract as much liquid as possible.
3. Whisk eggs, flour, cilantro, chile, cumin, and pepper in a large mixing bowl. Add sweet potato mixture, and stir well.
4. Heat oil in a heavy, large skillet over medium-high heat. Add batter by ¼-cup measures, and flatten pancakes with a slotted spatula. Cook for 4 minutes, or until browned and crisp. Turn gently with a slotted spatula, and fry the other side. Remove pancakes from the skillet, and drain on paper towels. Place pancakes in the warm oven with the door ajar, and repeat with remaining batter.

5. To serve, spread tops of pancakes with sour cream and then top with salsa. Serve immediately.

Note: The batter can be prepared up to 6 hours in advance and refrigerated, tightly covered. Also, the pancakes can be made up to 1 day in advance, and reheated in a 375°F oven for 8–10 minutes, or until hot and crispy.

Each serving contains:

157 MG SODIUM | 429 calories | 225 calories from fat | 25 g fat | 6 g saturated fat | 7 g protein | 46 g carbohydrates

Variation:

- For more all-American flavor, omit the cilantro, chiles, and cumin; add 2 tablespoons firmly packed dark brown sugar and 1 teaspoon ground cinnamon to the recipe. Substitute applesauce for the salsa to top the sour cream.

When using a food processor for pureeing food, never fill it more than ⅔ of the way up so there's room for the food to move. But when you're chopping food finely it needs a lot more space than that. Don't fill it more than ¼ full, or the food on the bottom will puree while the food on top does not chop.

Samosa Patties

Samosas are small Indian appetizers usually fried in pastry. These colorful and flavorful patties have all the requisite flavors, with far less fuss. The simple yogurt sauce flecked with tomatoes moistens them nicely.

Yield: 6 servings | **Active time:** 20 minutes | **Start to finish:** 1½ hours, including 1 hour for chilling

SAUCE

1 cup plain yogurt
2 tablespoons lemon juice
2 ripe plum tomatoes, rinsed, cored, seeded, and chopped

PATTIES

2 large eggs, lightly beaten
½ cup all-purpose flour
¼ cup chopped fresh cilantro
2 jalapeño or serrano chiles, seeds and ribs removed, and finely chopped
3 garlic cloves, peeled and minced
1 tablespoon grated fresh ginger
2 teaspoons ground cumin
1 cup fresh corn kernels or frozen corn kernels, thawed
2 medium carrots, scrubbed and grated
1 large russet potato, peeled and grated
½ cup frozen peas, thawed
Freshly ground black pepper to taste
¼ cup vegetable oil

1. Place yogurt in a sieve over a mixing bowl, and allow it to drain for 1 hour. Discard whey, and stir in lemon juice and tomatoes. Refrigerate until ready to use.
2. Combine eggs, flour, cilantro, chiles, garlic, ginger, and cumin in a mixing bowl. Whisk well. Stir in corn, carrots, potato, and peas, and season to taste with pepper.
3. Divide mixture into 12 portions, and form each into a patty ¾ inch thick. Refrigerate patties for 1 hour.

4. Preheat the oven to 200°F, and line a baking sheet with aluminum foil.

5. Heat oil in a large skillet over medium-high heat. Add patties, being careful not to crowd the pan; this may have to be done in batches. Cook patties for 5 minutes per side, or until browned. Remove patties from the skillet, and drain on paper towels. Place patties in the warm oven with the door ajar, and repeat with remaining patties. Serve immediately, passing sauce separately.

Note: The batter can be prepared up to 6 hours in advance and refrigerated, tightly covered. Also, the pancakes can be made up to 1 day in advance, and reheated in a 375°F oven for 8–10 minutes, or until hot and crispy.

Each serving contains:

78 MG SODIUM | 224 calories | 83 calories from fat | 9 g fat | 2 g saturated fat | 8 g protein | 29 g carbohydrates

The practice of draining yogurt to remove much of its liquid is a good one for any yogurt-based dip or sauce. It creates a sauce with the texture of sour cream, which doesn't overly moisten food.

Sautéed Pinto Bean Cakes

These cakes are similar in flavor to refried beans, but in addition to being low in sodium, they're also much lower in fat than refried beans. The exterior of the patties is crisp, while the center is creamy. Serve them with some stir-fried vegetables.

Yield: 6 servings | **Active time:** 20 minutes | **Start to finish:** 20 minutes

5 tablespoons olive oil, divided
1 medium onion, peeled and coarsely chopped
3 garlic cloves, peeled and minced
2 jalapeño or serrano chiles, seeds and ribs removed, and diced
2 tablespoons chili powder
1½ tablespoons ground cumin
3 cups cooked pinto beans
½ cup chopped fresh cilantro
½ cup water
Cayenne to taste
1 cup Summer Tomato Salsa (recipe on page 68) (optional)

1. Preheat the oven to 200°F, and line a baking sheet with aluminum foil.
2. Heat 2 tablespoons oil in a large skillet over medium-high heat, swirling to coat the pan. Add onion, garlic, and chiles, and cook, stirring frequently, for 3 minutes, or until onion is translucent. Add chili powder and cumin, and cook, stirring constantly, for 1 minute. Add beans, cilantro, and water. Bring to a boil and simmer mixture, stirring frequently, for 3 minutes.
3. Transfer mixture to a food processor fitted with the steel blade and puree. Scrape mixture into a mixing bowl, and season to taste with cayenne. Divide mixture into 12 parts, forming each into a patty ¼ inch thick.
4. Heat remaining oil in a heavy, large skillet over high heat, swirling to coat the pan. Add bean cakes, and cook for 1–2 minutes per side, or until crisp, turning gently with a slotted spatula. Remove patties from the skillet and drain on paper towels. Place patties in the warm oven with the door ajar, and repeat with remaining patties. To serve, place 2 cakes on each plate, and top each with tomato salsa, if using. Serve immediately.

Note: The bean mixture can be made up to 1 day in advance and refrigerated, tightly covered. Fry the cakes just prior to serving.

Each serving contains:

29.5 MG SODIUM | 221 calories | 90 calories from fat | 10 g fat | 1 g saturated fat | 8 g protein | 26 g carbohydrates

Variation:

- Substitute black beans or kidney beans for the pinto beans.

A chile pepper's seeds and ribs contain almost all of the capsaicin, the chemical compound that delivers the pepper's punch. Since small chiles have proportionately more seeds and ribs to flesh, a general rule is the smaller the chile, the hotter the pepper.

Vegetable and Brown Rice Loaf

The nutty flavor of brown rice is enlivened with a large range of colorful and healthful vegetables in this vegetarian version of a meatloaf. The slices are then topped with tomato sauce, and your meal is complete.

Yield: 6 servings | **Active time:** 20 minutes | **Start to finish:** 1¾ hours

³/₄ cup brown rice

2 cups water

2 teaspoons dried thyme

4 garlic cloves, peeled and minced, divided

Freshly ground black pepper to taste

2 small yellow squash, rinsed, trimmed, and coarsely grated

3 tablespoons olive oil

8 scallions, white parts and 3 inches of green tops, rinsed, trimmed, and thinly sliced

2 carrots, peeled and grated

2 large eggs, lightly beaten

¼ cup chopped fresh parsley

½ cup crumbled feta cheese

1 tablespoon herbes de Provence

1½ cups Low-Sodium Marinara Sauce (recipe on page 54) (optional)

Vegetable oil spray

1. Rinse rice in a sieve, and place it in a saucepan. Add water, thyme, 2 garlic cloves, and pepper, and bring to a boil over high heat, stirring occasionally. Reduce the heat to low, cover the pan, and cook rice for 40–45 minutes, or until tender and the liquid is absorbed. Check rice after 30 minutes to see if more water is needed. Fluff rice with a fork.

2. Place yellow squash in a colander, and allow it to drain for 30 minutes. Wring it out in a cloth tea towel.

3. While rice cooks, heat oil in a skillet over medium-high heat. Add scallions, remaining garlic, and carrots. Cook, stirring frequently, for 5 minutes, or until vegetables soften. Beat eggs with parsley, cheese, and herbes de Provence. Stir in vegetables, cooked rice, and yellow squash. Season to taste with pepper.

4. Preheat the oven to 375°F, line a 9 x 5-inch loaf pan with heavy-duty aluminum foil, and grease the foil with vegetable oil spray. Bring a kettle of water to a boil.

5. Scrape the vegetable and rice mixture into the prepared pan, smoothing the top. Cover the pan with foil, and place the loaf pan into a baking pan. Pour boiling water into the baking pan halfway up the sides of the loaf pan.

6. Bake for 50–60 minutes, or until set. Allow loaf to rest for 10 minutes, then unmold onto a platter, and serve immediately, topped with marinara sauce, if using.

Note: The loaf can be prepared for baking up to 1 day in advance and refrigerated, tightly covered. It can also be baked up to 2 days in advance. Reheat it unmolded in a 350°F oven for 25–35 minutes, covered with foil, or until hot.

Each serving contains:

173 MG SODIUM | 198 calories | 86 calories from fat | 9 g fat | 2.5 g saturated fat | 8 g protein | 22.5 g carbohydrates

Variation:

- Substitute zucchini for the yellow squash and substitute Italian seasoning for the herbes de Provence.

A casserole surrounded by boiling water is called a *bain marie* (pronounced *bahn mahree*) in classic French cooking. Because water reaches only 212°F, it creates a gentle heat around food in the oven, and keeps the exterior from becoming crusty.

Vegetarian Chili with Bulgur

Bulgur, an ancient grain, has a nutty flavor and "meaty" texture after it's cooked. It makes a great addition to this hearty chili.

Yield: 6 servings | **Active time:** 15 minutes | **Start to finish:** 35 minutes

   2 tablespoons olive oil
   1 large onion, peeled and chopped
   5 garlic cloves, peeled and minced
   2 carrots, peeled and chopped
   1 green bell pepper, seeds and ribs removed, and chopped
   2 jalapeño or serrano chiles, seeds and ribs removed, and finely
     chopped
   2 tablespoons chili powder
   1 tablespoon smoked Spanish paprika
   1 tablespoon ground cumin
   1½ teaspoons dried oregano
   2 (14.5-ounce) cans no-salt-added diced tomatoes
   2 (8-ounce) cans no-salt-added tomato sauce
   ½ cup bulgur
   4 cups cooked kidney beans
   Freshly ground black pepper to taste
   3 cups cooked brown rice, hot

1. Heat olive oil in a saucepan over medium-high heat. Add onion and garlic, and cook, stirring frequently, for 3 minutes, or until onion is translucent. Add carrots, green pepper, and chiles, and cook for 2 minutes. Add chili powder, paprika, cumin, and oregano, and cook for 1 minute, stirring constantly.

2. Add tomatoes, tomato sauce, and bulgur. Bring to a boil, reduce the heat to medium, and cook, uncovered, for 20 minutes, or until bulgur is tender, stirring occasionally. Add beans, and simmer 5 minutes. Season to taste with pepper, and serve immediately over rice.

Note: The dish can be made up to 2 days in advance and refrigerated, tightly covered. Reheat it, covered, over low heat, stirring occasionally, until hot.

Each serving contains:

103 MG SODIUM | 305 calories | 42 calories from fat | 5 g fat | 1 g saturated fat | 15 g protein | 54 g carbohydrates

Garlicky Kale and Garbanzo Beans

Kale is a member of the cabbage family, and its flavor is rather mild and non-bitter for a vegetable classified as a green. This is a quick and easy recipe, and serving it over brown rice adds to the nutritional content.

Yield: 6 servings | **Active time:** 15 minutes | **Start to finish:** 25 minutes

1½ pounds kale
¼ cup olive oil
5 garlic cloves, peeled and thinly sliced
½–¾ teaspoon crushed red pepper flakes
1 cup Vegetable Stock (recipe on page 28)
1½ cups cooked garbanzo beans
2 tablespoons balsamic vinegar
3 cups cooked brown rice, hot

1. Rinse kale and discard thick stems. Slice leaves into 1-inch ribbons.
2. Heat oil in a large covered skillet over medium-high heat. Add garlic and red pepper flakes, and cook for 1 minute, stirring constantly. Add kale by large handfuls, turning with tongs until wilted before adding next addition.
3. Add stock, and cook for 3 minutes, until greens are all wilted. Add beans, cover the pan, and cook for 3–5 minutes, or until kale is tender. Sprinkle with vinegar, and serve immediately over rice.

Note: The dish can be prepared except for sprinkling with vinegar 1 day in advance and refrigerated, tightly covered. Reheat it, covered, over medium heat, then sprinkle with vinegar.

Each serving contains:

58 MG SODIUM | 200 calories | 82 calories from fat | 9 g fat | 1 g saturated fat | 8 g protein | 25 g carbohydrates

Variation:
- Substitute broccoli rabe for the kale.

Lentil and Zucchini Curry

Healthful lentils, called *dal* in Indian cooking, are one of the few dried legumes that need no pre-soaking, so this flavorful dish is quickly on your dinner table. Serve it on top of some basmati rice, with a tossed salad on the side.

Yield: 6 servings | **Active time:** 15 minutes | **Start to finish:** 55 minutes

¼ cup vegetable oil

2 onions, peeled and chopped

3 garlic cloves, peeled and minced

1 jalapeño or serrano chile, seeds and ribs removed, and finely chopped

1 tablespoon curry powder

1 teaspoon ground cumin

1 teaspoon ground coriander

½ teaspoon ground ginger

2 medium tomatoes, rinsed, cored, seeded, and chopped

1½ cups brown lentils, picked over and rinsed well

4 cups Vegetable Stock (recipe on page 28)

2 (3-inch) cinnamon sticks

3 medium zucchini, rinsed, trimmed, and cut into ½-inch dice

¼ cup chopped fresh cilantro

Freshly ground black pepper to taste

3 cups cooked basmati rice, hot

1. Heat oil in a Dutch oven over medium-high heat. Add onion, garlic, and chile, and cook, stirring frequently, for 3 minutes, or until onion is translucent. Stir in curry powder, cumin, coriander, and ginger. Cook for 1 minute, stirring constantly.

2. Add tomatoes, lentils, stock, and cinnamon sticks to the pan, and bring to a boil over medium-high heat. Reduce the heat to low, and simmer mixture, uncovered, adding more stock if necessary to keep ingredients just covered with liquid, for 25–35 minutes, or until lentils soften.

3. Remove and discard cinnamon sticks, and add zucchini to the pan. Cover the pan, and cook for 10 minutes, or until zucchini is tender. Stir in cilantro, season to taste with pepper, and serve immediately over rice.

Note: The dish can be cooked up to 2 days in advance and refrigerated, tightly covered. Reheat it over low heat, stirring occasionally, until hot.

Each serving contains:

34 MG SODIUM | 287 calories | 74 calories from fat | 8 g fat | 1 g saturated fat | 15 g protein | 41 g carbohydrates

Variation:
- Substitute yellow squash or green bell pepper for the zucchini.

Always buy curry powder in small jars, because its life is only about 2 months, rather than the 6 months of many other spices. This ground blend, made up of up to 20 herbs and spices, loses its flavor and aroma very quickly.

Chapter 6:
Aquatic Adventures

All species of fin fish can be part of a low-sodium diet, and luckily many species are now nationally accessible at a relatively low cost. While fish is usually higher in price than most meats, there is no waste to a fish fillet, and with its low fat content it doesn't shrink the way that meats do. So the price per edible ounce of fish is really about the same as for other forms of protein like a chuck roast or pork loin, if still more expensive than a chicken.

There are fabulous recipes for fish in the world's cuisines. European cooks realized centuries ago that a sprinkling with lemon juice or another acid brightens the flavors of fish, even if they were hardly concerned with sodium.

I also realize that many people who enjoy fish don't enjoy "fishy" flavor. But there's a way around that for these recipes. Rather than using the seafood stock specified, substitute vegetable or chicken stock. The "fishy" quotient will be greatly diminished.

CHOOSING THE CHOICEST

It's more important to use the freshest fish—and one that is reasonably priced—than any specific fish; that's why these recipes are not written for cod, halibut, or pompano. They're written for two generic types of fish—thin white-fleshed fillets and thick white-fleshed fillets. These encompass most types of fish.

They are all low in fat, mild to delicate in flavor, and flake easily when cooked. The only species of fish that should *not* be used in these recipes are tuna, bluefish, and mackerel; they will all be too strong. Salmon, if you find it at a good price, can be substituted for either classification of fish, depending on the thickness of the fillet.

There are thousands of species that fit these rather large definitions. Here are some of the most common:

- **Thin fillets:** Flounder, sole, perch, red snapper, trout, tilapia, ocean perch, catfish, striped bass, turbot, and whitefish.

- **Thick fillets:** Halibut, scrod, grouper, sea bass, mahi-mahi, pompano, yellowtail, swordfish, cod, and haddock.

FISH FACTS

Fish are high in protein and low to moderate in fat, cholesterol, and sodium. A 3-ounce portion of fish has between 15 and 70 mg of sodium, and between 47 and 170 calories depending on the species. Fish is an excellent source of B vitamins, iodine, phosphorus, potassium, iron, and calcium.

Mollusks and crustaceans, however, are higher in sodium. But they're also so much higher in price that they don't fit within the strictures of a *$3 Meals* book. For example, a 3-ounce portion of mussels contains 252 mg of sodium, and the same size portion of Alaskan king crab has a whopping 700 mg of sodium.

The most important nutrient in fish may be the omega-3 fatty acids. These are the primary polyunsaturated fatty acids found in the fat and oils of fish. They have been found to lower the levels of low-density lipoproteins (LDL), the "bad" cholesterol, and raise the levels of high-density lipoproteins (HDL), the "good" cholesterol. Fatty fish that live in cold water, such as mackerel and salmon, seem to have the most omega-3 fatty acids, although all fish have some.

HANDLING THE AQUATICS

Most supermarkets still display fish on chipped ice in a case rather than pre-packaging it, and they should. Fish should be kept at even a lower temperature than meats. Fish fillets or steaks should look bright, lustrous, and moist, with no signs of discoloration or drying.

When making your fish selection, keep a few simple guidelines in mind: above all, do not buy any fish that actually smells fishy, indicating that it is no longer fresh or it hasn't been cut or stored properly. Fresh fish has the mild, clean scent of the sea—nothing more. Look for bright, shiny colors in the fish scales, because as a fish sits, its skin becomes more pale and dull looking. Then peer into the eyes; they should be black and beady. If they're milky or sunken, the fish has been dead too long. And if the fish isn't behind glass, gently poke its flesh. If the indentation remains, the fish is old.

Rinse all fish under cold running water before cutting it or cooking it. With fillets, run your fingers in every direction along the top of the fillet before cooking, and feel for any pesky little bones.

You can remove bones easily in two ways. Larger bones will come out if they're stroked with a vegetable peeler, and you can pull out smaller bones with tweezers. This is not a long process, but it's a gesture that will be greatly appreciated by all who eat the fish.

SEAFOOD STRATEGIES

Fish does not freeze well—either before or after cooking. The reason is that when food is frozen the liquid inside the cells expands to form ice. This expansion punctures the delicate cell walls, which makes the fish mushy once thawed.

Maybe fish doesn't freeze well, but there's no need to freeze it because it cooks so quickly. It's the stew bases and sauces that take the time, so my suggestion is to double or even triple the recipe for that component of a dish, and freeze the extra portions. Thaw it when you come home, add the fresh fish, and within 10 minutes you'll be enjoying a delicious meal with perfectly cooked fish. The fish can even be of a different species, depending on what you find in the market that day.

TALKING TUNA

While canned tuna is listed along with other canned fish on the "Foods to Forget" section in Chapter 2, many national processors do have a low-sodium option, although I couldn't find a generic store brand at a lower cost with a low-sodium option, either in stores or on Web sites.

The amount of sodium in low-sodium tuna is inconsistent; it depends on the brand. If you want tuna salad for lunch, take your reading glasses with you to the supermarket.

There are health concerns as well as cost reasons for specifying light tuna rather than white tuna, sometimes called albacore tuna, in these recipes. White tuna has been found to be much higher in mercury than light tuna, so light tuna is better on both scores.

Spanish Fish

It doesn't get much easier than this recipe; there are just a few ingredients and it's on the table in a matter of minutes. I usually serve it over rice to enjoy every drop of the garlicky sauce.

Yield: 6 servings | **Active time:** 15 minutes | **Start to finish:** 15 minutes

1½ pounds thick white-fleshed fish fillets
½ cup olive oil
6 garlic cloves, peeled and minced
2 tablespoons smoked Spanish paprika
3 tablespoons chopped fresh parsley
3 tablespoons lemon juice
Crushed red pepper flakes to taste
3 cups cooked brown or white rice, hot

1. Rinse fish, pat dry with paper towels, and cut fish into ¾-inch cubes.
2. Heat oil in a large skillet over medium-high heat. Add garlic and paprika, and cook for 1 minute, stirring constantly. Add fish and parsley, and cook for 2 minutes, uncovered, or until fish is opaque. Sprinkle fish with lemon juice, and season to taste with red pepper flakes. Serve immediately over rice.

Note: The fish can be prepared up to 3 hours in advance and served at room temperature.

Each serving contains:

63 MG SODIUM | 259 calories | 153 calories from fat | 17 g fat | 2 g saturated fat | 24 g protein | 2 g carbohydrates

Variation:

- Substitute ¾-inch cubes of boneless, skinless chicken breast or chicken thighs for the fish. Cook chicken for 3-5 minutes, or until chicken is cooked through and no longer pink.

Zesty Mediterranean Fish Stew

There's a hint of sweet orange balancing the wine and tomatoes in this easy fish stew seasoned with the sunny flavors of Provence. Serve it with slices of toast in the bottom of the bowl to absorb the juices, and a tossed salad.

Yield: 6 servings | **Active time:** 25 minutes | **Start to finish:** 55 minutes

    1 juice orange
    3 tablespoons olive oil
    1 medium onion, peeled and diced
    3 garlic cloves, peeled and minced
    1 small fennel bulb, rinsed trimmed, cored, and diced
    1 cup dry white wine
    1½ cups Seafood Stock (recipe on page 29)
    2 (14.5-ounce) cans no-salt-added diced tomatoes, undrained
    2 tablespoons no-salt-added tomato paste
    2 tablespoons chopped fresh parsley
    1 teaspoon dried thyme
    1 bay leaf
    ½ teaspoon crushed red pepper flakes, or to taste
    1½ pounds thick white-fleshed fish fillets, rinsed and cut into 1-inch
      cubes
    Freshly ground black pepper to taste

1. Grate zest from orange, and squeeze juice from fruit. Set aside.
2. Heat oil in a 4-quart saucepan over medium-high heat. Add onion, garlic, and fennel, and cook, stirring frequently, for 3 minutes, or until onion is translucent. Add wine, and cook for 3 minutes.
3. Add orange juice, orange zest, stock, tomatoes, tomato paste, parsley, thyme, bay leaf, and crushed red pepper flakes. Bring to a boil over medium-high heat, stirring occasionally. Reduce the heat to low, and simmer soup, covered, for 15–20 minutes, or until vegetables soften.
4. Add fish, cover the pan again, and cook for 3–5 minutes, or until fish is cooked and flakes easily. Remove and discard bay leaf, and season to taste with pepper. Serve immediately.

Note: The soup base can be prepared up to 2 days in advance and refrigerated, tightly covered. Reheat it, covered, over low heat, stirring frequently until it comes to a boil, and then add and cook the fish.

Each serving contains:

143 MG SODIUM | 242 calories | 65 calories from fat | 7 g fat | 1 g saturated fat | 22 g protein | 14 g carbohydrates

Variation:

- Substitute red wine for the white wine.

While the green stalks attached to the fennel bulb aren't used in cooking, there's no reason to discard them. Use them as a substitute for celery to add crunch to salads. They have more flavor than celery, too.

Caribbean Curried Fish Stew with Sweet Potatoes

The spiciness of the curry powder and chile is tamed by creamy coconut milk in this Caribbean-flavored dish. With vegetables and sweet potatoes included in the recipe, this qualifies as a one-dish meal.

Yield: 6 servings | **Active time:** 20 minutes | **Start to finish:** 45 minutes

2 tablespoons vegetable oil

1 small onion, peeled and chopped

4 garlic cloves, peeled and minced

2 jalapeño or serrano chiles, seeds and ribs removed, and chopped

3 tablespoons curry powder

$\frac{1}{2}$ teaspoon ground cinnamon

Pinch of ground allspice

$\frac{1}{2}$ cup Seafood Stock (recipe on page 29)

3 tablespoons peanut butter

1 (15-ounce) can light coconut milk

1 teaspoon granulated sugar

2 large carrots, peeled and cut into $\frac{1}{2}$-inch slices

1 large sweet potato, peeled and cut into $\frac{1}{2}$-inch dice

$1\frac{1}{2}$ pounds thick white-fleshed fish fillets, rinsed and cut into 1-inch cubes

Freshly ground black pepper to taste

$\frac{1}{4}$ cup chopped fresh cilantro

1. Heat oil in a deep skillet over medium-high heat. Add onion, garlic, and chiles, and cook, stirring frequently, for 3 minutes, or until onion is translucent. Add curry powder, cinnamon, and allspice and cook for 1 minute, stirring constantly. Scrape mixture into a food processor fitted with the steel blade or into a blender. Add stock and peanut butter, and puree until smooth.

2. Return puree to the skillet, and add coconut milk and sugar. Bring to a boil over medium-high heat, stirring occasionally. Add carrots and sweet potato, and bring to a boil. Reduce the heat to low, cover the pan, and simmer for 12–15 minutes, or until vegetables are tender.

3. Add fish to the pan, and cook for 3–5 minutes, or until fish is cooked through and flakes easily. Season to taste with pepper, and serve immediately, sprinkling each serving with cilantro.

Note: The dish can be prepared up to 1 day in advance and refrigerated, tightly covered. Reheat it over low heat, covered, until hot, stirring occasionally.

Each serving contains:

144 MG SODIUM | 291 calories | 134 calories from fat | 15 g fat | 5 g saturated fat | 23.5 g protein | 14.5 g carbohydrates

Variation:

- Substitute chicken stock for the seafood stock, and substitute 1¼ pounds boneless, skinless chicken breast, cut into 1-inch cubes, for the fish. Add the chicken to the stew along with the carrots and sweet potatoes.

Never substitute bottled clam juice for seafood stock in recipes because clam juice, like clams themselves, is very high in sodium. A ¼ cup serving contains between 120 mg and 280 mg, depending on the brand.

Seafood Gumbo

Gumbo is a classic dish from the Louisiana bayous; the name comes from the African word for okra, which is used as the thickening agent. This version is only mildly spicy, but feel free to add more crushed red pepper flakes if you like fiery flavors; serve it over rice.

Yield: 6 servings | **Active time:** 15 minutes | **Start to finish:** 1 hour

½ cup vegetable oil

¾ cup all-purpose flour

2 tablespoons unsalted butter

1 large onion, peeled and diced

1 large green bell pepper, seeds and ribs removed, and diced

2 celery ribs, rinsed, trimmed, and diced

5 garlic cloves, peeled and minced

4 cups Seafood Stock (recipe on page 29)

1 teaspoon dried thyme

2 bay leaves

1 (14.5-ounce) can no-salt-added diced tomatoes, undrained

½ teaspoon crushed red pepper flakes, or to taste

1 (1-pound) bag frozen sliced okra, thawed

1½ pounds thick white-fleshed fish fillets, rinsed and cut into ¾-inch cubes

3 tablespoons chopped fresh parsley

Freshly ground black pepper to taste

3 cups cooked white or brown rice, hot

1. Preheat the oven to 450°F. Combine oil and flour in a Dutch oven, and place the pan in the oven. Bake roux for 20–30 minutes, or until walnut brown, stirring occasionally.

2. While roux bakes, heat butter in large skillet over medium-high heat. Add onion, green pepper, celery, and garlic. Cook, stirring frequently, for 3 minutes, or until onion is translucent. Set aside.

3. Remove roux from the oven, and place the pan on the stove over medium heat. Add stock and whisk constantly until mixture comes to a boil and thickens. Add vegetable mixture, thyme, bay leaves, tomatoes, and red pepper flakes to the pan. Bring to a boil, cover, and cook over low heat for 20 minutes, stirring occasionally. Add okra, and cook for an additional 10 minutes, or until okra is very tender.

4. Add fish and parsley. Bring back to a boil and cook, covered, over low heat for 3–5 minutes, or until fish is opaque and cooked through. Remove and discard bay leaves, season to taste with pepper, and serve immediately over rice.

Note: The dish can be prepared up to 2 days in advance and refrigerated, tightly covered. Reheat it, covered, over low heat, stirring occasionally.

Each serving contains:

154 MG SODIUM | 536 calories | 218 calories from fat | 24 g fat | 5 g saturated fat | 28 g protein | 49 g carbohydrates

Variation:
- Substitute 1½ pounds boneless, skinless chicken meat for the fish, and chicken stock for the seafood stock.

Roux, pronounced *roo*, as in kangaroo, is a mixture of fat and flour used as a thickening agent for soups and sauces. The first step in all roux is to cook the flour, so that the dish doesn't taste like library paste. For white sauces, this is done over low heat and the fat used is butter. Many Creole and Cajun dishes, such as gumbo, use a fuller-flavored brown roux made with oil or drippings and cooked until deep brown. The dark roux gives dishes an almost nutty flavor.

Crunchy Southern Fish

You'll notice that breadcrumbs are not mentioned in this book, and that's because it's almost impossible to find them without a high amount of sodium. But the good news is that cornmeal is a low-sodium food, and it produces a wonderful crispy crust for these fish fillets served with a variation on remoulade sauce. Serve them with coleslaw.

Yield: 6 servings | **Active time:** 25 minutes | **Start to finish:** 30 minutes

SAUCE

> 1/3 cup Low-Sodium Mayonnaise (recipe on page 39)
> 3 tablespoons no-salt-added ketchup
> 2 tablespoons chopped fresh parsley
> 2 tablespoons Marvelous Mustard (recipe on page 40)
> 2 tablespoons sweet pickle relish

FISH

> 1½ pounds thin white-fleshed fish fillets
> 2 large eggs, lightly beaten
> 2 tablespoons whole milk
> Freshly ground black pepper to taste
> ¾ cup yellow cornmeal
> ⅔ cup vegetable oil, divided

1. Preheat the oven to 200°F, and line a baking sheet with aluminum foil. For sauce, combine mayonnaise, ketchup, parsley, mustard, and pickle relish in a mixing bowl, and whisk well. Refrigerate until ready to serve.

2. Rinse fish and pat dry with paper towels. Cut fish into 2-inch sections. Place eggs in a shallow bowl, and beat with milk. Season to taste with pepper. Place cornmeal on a sheet of plastic wrap.

3. Heat 1/3 cup oil in a large skillet over medium-high heat. Dip ½ of fish pieces in egg mixture, allowing excess to drip back into the pan, and then into cornmeal. Fry fish for 2 minutes per side, turning it gently with a slotted spatula, or until fish is browned and crisp and flakes easily. Drain fish on paper towels, and keep warm in the oven. Discard oil from the skillet, wipe out the skillet with paper towels, and then fry remaining fish in remaining oil as detailed.

4. Serve immediately, passing sauce separately.

Note: The sauce can be prepared up to 2 days in advance and refrigerated, tightly covered.

Each serving contains:

106 MG SODIUM | 456 calories | 305 calories from fat | 34 g fat | 4 g saturated fat | 23 g protein | 16 g carbohydrates

Variations:
- Add $1/4$–$1/2$ teaspoon crushed red pepper flakes to the sauce for a spicier dish.
- Add $1/2$ cup finely chopped pecans to the cornmeal for the breading mixture.
- Substitute boneless, skinless chicken breast halves, pounded to an even thickness of $1/2$ inch between 2 sheets of plastic wrap, for the fish. Cook chicken for 3–4 minutes per side, or until chicken is cooked through and no longer pink.

It's not being wasteful to discard the fat and wipe out the pan between batches of fish. Foods such as cornmeal and nuts tend to burn easily, and the second batch of fish would be in danger of tasting burnt if cooked in the original oil.

Baked Fish with Tomatoes and Fennel

Fennel is a relatively inexpensive vegetable, and it's underutilized in cooking. It has the crunchy texture of celery, but a refreshing anise flavor. When combined with onion and tomatoes it becomes a fast and lean sauce for fish. Serve it with some brown rice braised in stock and a tossed salad.

Yield: 6 servings | **Active time:** 20 minutes | **Start to finish:** 35 minutes

¼ cup olive oil
1 large onion, peeled and thinly sliced
3 garlic cloves, peeled and minced
2 fennel bulbs, trimmed, cored, and thinly sliced
2 (14.5-ounce) cans no-salt-added diced tomatoes, drained
1 cup dry white wine
½ cup orange juice
2 bay leaves
Freshly ground black pepper to taste
1½ pounds thick white-fleshed fish fillets, rinsed and cut into serving-sized pieces
3 cups cooked brown rice, hot

1. Preheat the oven to 450°F, and grease a 9 x 13-inch baking pan.
2. Heat olive oil in a large saucepan over medium heat. Add onion and garlic, and cook, stirring frequently, for 3 minutes, or until onion is translucent. Add fennel, and cook for 2 minutes, stirring frequently. Add tomatoes, wine, orange juice, and bay leaves to the pan. Bring to a boil, reduce the heat to low, and simmer mixture, uncovered, for 15 minutes, stirring occasionally. Season to taste with pepper.
3. Transfer vegetable mixture to the prepared pan. Sprinkle fish with pepper, and place fish on top of the vegetables. Bake fish for 10–15 minutes, or until fish is opaque. Remove and discard bay leaves, and serve immediately over rice.

Note: The vegetable mixture can be prepared up to 2 days in advance and refrigerated, tightly covered. Reheat it over low heat to a simmer before baking the fish.

Each serving contains:

156 MG SODIUM | 258 calories | 74 calories from fat | 8 g fat | 1 g saturated fat | 23 g protein | 17 g carbohydrates

Variation:
- Substitute slices of light firm tofu for the fish.

When cooking fish dishes, it's important that the vegetables are hot. If you add chilled veggies to fish, it will be overcooked by the time the vegetables are hot.

Fish in White Wine Sauce with Oranges

Like most fish dishes, this one is on the table quickly, and the combination of the sweet orange with herbs and tomatoes makes it especially attractive. Serve it with a tossed salad and some whole-wheat pasta.

Yield: 6 servings | **Active time:** 20 minutes | **Start to finish:** 35 minutes

3 tablespoons olive oil

3 scallions, white parts and 3 inches of green tops, rinsed, trimmed, and thinly sliced

1 celery rib, rinsed, trimmed, and sliced

3 garlic cloves, peeled and minced

1 (16-ounce) package frozen pearl onions, thawed

1 (14.5-ounce) can no-salt-added diced tomatoes, drained

1/4 cup chopped fresh parsley

1 1/2 cups Seafood Stock (recipe on page 29)

1/2 cup dry white wine

1 cup orange juice

1 bay leaf

1 1/2 pounds thick white-fleshed fish fillets, cut into 6 pieces and rinsed

2 navel oranges, rind and white pith removed, and cut into 1/2-inch cubes

1 (10-ounce) package frozen cut green beans, thawed

Freshly ground black pepper to taste

1. Heat olive oil in a large skillet over medium-high heat. Add scallions, celery, and garlic, and cook, stirring frequently, for 3 minutes, or until scallions are translucent. Add pearl onions, tomatoes, parsley, stock, white wine, orange juice, and bay leaf to the skillet. Bring to a boil and simmer, uncovered, for 3 minutes.

2. Add fish and orange pieces to the skillet. Cover, bring to a boil, reduce the heat to low, and cook for 5 minutes. Turn fish gently with a slotted spatula, add green beans, and cook for an additional 5 minutes. Season to taste with pepper. To serve, place fish on plates and surround each portion with vegetables. Serve immediately.

Note: The dish can be cooked up to 1 day in advance and refrigerated, tightly covered. Reheat it, covered, over low heat.

Each serving contains:

152 MG SODIUM | 308 calories | 75 calories from fat | 8 g fat | 1 g saturated fat | 25 g protein | 29.5 g carbohydrates

Variation:
- Substitute boneless, skinless chicken breast halves, pounded to an even thickness of $1/2$ inch, for the fish. Cook chicken for 10–12 minutes, or until cooked through and no longer pink.

Here's an easy way to cut the oranges; rather than peel them, cut a small slice off both ends so it will sit firmly on the cutting board, and then cut down the sides to remove both the rind and pith in one operation.

Seafood "Sausages"

The food processor reinvented cooking for almost everyone I know; mine has a dedicated corner in the dishwasher because I use it daily. With the food processor you can make this pureed fish mixture quickly. Then poach it into sausage shapes and top it with a tomato sauce.

Yield: 8 servings | **Active time:** 20 minutes | **Start to finish:** 45 minutes

1½ pounds white-fleshed fish fillet, cut into 1-inch pieces
2 large egg whites
¼ cup half-and-half
2 tablespoons chopped fresh parsley
1 teaspoon herbes de Provence
½ pound salmon fillet, skinned and finely chopped
Freshly ground black pepper to taste
1½ cups Low-Sodium Marinara Sauce (recipe on page 54) or
   purchased marinara sauce, heated
Vegetable oil spray

1. Bring a large pot of water to a boil. Cut 12 (1-foot-square) pieces of aluminum foil. Set aside.
2. Combine fish, egg whites, half-and-half, parsley, and herbes de Provence in a food processor fitted with the steel blade. Puree until smooth, and scrape mixture into a mixing bowl. Stir salmon into the mixture, and season to taste with pepper.
3. Lightly grease one side of each foil square with vegetable oil spray. Place a spoonful of sausage mixture on one side and form into a cylinder with your fingers. Roll the foil, twisting the ends to seal the packages tightly. Repeat until all sausages are formed.
4. Add sausage packages to the boiling water, and regulate the heat so that they are just simmering. Cover the pot, and simmer sausages for 15 minutes.
5. Remove sausages from water with tongs, and allow them to rest for 10 minutes. Gently unwrap sausages over the sink, allowing any water that has seeped in to drain. Serve immediately, topped with tomato sauce.

Note: The sausages can be cooked up to 1 day in advance and refrigerated, tightly covered. Reheat them, covered, in a 325°F oven for 10–12 minutes, or until hot.

Each serving contains:

96 MG SODIUM | 194 calories | 75 calories from fat | 8 g fat | 2 g saturated fat | 23 g protein | 4 g carbohydrates

Variation:

- Substitute any finely chopped fish or shellfish—such as scallops or shrimp—for the salmon. It's nice to have the other fish be of a contrasting color.

> This method of poaching can be used for any meat loaf or sausage mixture too. For poultry or meats, make sure that the rolls have been cooked to 165°F.

Tunisian Fish

Many North African dishes are served with a spicy condiment called harissa, which is a blending of chiles and spices along with bell peppers. The succulent sauce served on these fillets is a low-sodium variation on that theme. Serve the dish with couscous and a tossed salad.

Yield: 6 servings | **Active time:** 20 minutes | **Start to finish:** 30 minutes

>   2 green bell peppers, seeds and ribs removed, and quartered
>   2 jalapeño or serrano chiles
>   3 garlic cloves, unpeeled
>   1/3 cup olive oil, divided
>   1 tablespoon ground cumin, divided
>   1 tablespoon ground coriander, divided
>   1 1/2 pounds thin white-fleshed fish fillets
>   3 tablespoons lemon juice, or to taste
>   Freshly ground black pepper to taste

1. Preheat the oven broiler, and line a broiler pan with heavy-duty aluminum foil.
2. Broil green bell peppers, chiles, and garlic cloves for 5–6 minutes per side, or until peppers are charred. Place mixture into a heavy resealable plastic bag, and cool for 5 minutes. (The plastic bag keeps in the steam, so the skin separates more easily.) Discard charred skin from peppers, chiles, and garlic; discard caps from chiles.
3. Combine peppers, chiles, garlic, 1/4 cup oil, 2 teaspoons cumin, and 2 teaspoons coriander in a food processor fitted with the steel blade or in a blender. Puree until smooth, and scrape into a small bowl.
4. Rinse fish and pat dry with paper towels. Sprinkle fish with remaining cumin and coriander.
5. Heat remaining oil in a large skillet over medium-high heat. Cook fish for 1 1/2–2 minutes per side, turning it gently with a spatula. Sprinkle fish with lemon juice and season to taste with pepper. Serve immediately, passing sauce separately.

Note: The sauce can be made up to 2 days in advance and refrigerated, tightly covered. Allow it to reach room temperature before serving.

Each serving contains:

64 MG SODIUM | 187 calories | 89 calories from fat | 10 g fat | 1 g saturated fat | 21 g protein | 3 g carbohydrates

Sautéed Fish with Citrus-Mustard Sauce

The bright flavors of orange juice and lemon juice and the sharp taste of mustard become a yin-yang of elements flavoring this easy and quick fish dish. Serve it with some braised rice, and a steamed green vegetable.

Yield: 6 servings | **Active time:** 15 minutes | **Start to finish:** 35 minutes

1½ pounds thin white-fleshed fish fillets
½ cup all-purpose flour
Freshly ground black pepper to taste
4 tablespoons (½ stick) unsalted butter
1 small onion, peeled and finely chopped
½ cup dry white wine
½ cup orange juice
¼ cup lemon juice
3 tablespoons chopped fresh parsley
2 tablespoons Marvelous Mustard (recipe on page 40)
1 teaspoon dried thyme

1. Rinse fish and pat dry with paper towels. Cut fish into 2-inch-wide strips. Combine flour and pepper in a shallow bowl, and dredge fish slices in flour, shaking off any excess over the sink.

2. Heat butter in a large skillet over medium-high heat. Add fish strips, and cook for 2–3 minutes per side, turning them gently with a slotted spatula. Remove fish from the skillet, and set aside.

3. Add onion to the skillet, and cook, stirring frequently, for 3 minutes, or until onion is translucent. Add wine, increase the heat to high, and cook for 3 minutes, or until wine has almost evaporated. Add orange juice, lemon juice, parsley, mustard, and thyme to the skillet, and stir well. Reduce the heat to medium, and simmer sauce, uncovered, for 5 minutes.

4. Return fish to the skillet to warm, and serve immediately.

Note: The dish can be prepared up to 3 hours in advance. Do not return the fish to the skillet to warm until just prior to serving.

Each serving contains:

65 MG SODIUM | 219 calories | 77 calories from fat | 9 g fat | 5 g saturated fat | 21 g protein | 10 g carbohydrates

Easy Italian Fish

While stir-frying is one of the ancient Chinese cooking methods, it's been adapted in the last few decades for dishes with clearly Western flavors, such as this fast and easy fish dish. Serve it over pasta with a tossed salad, and your meal is complete.

Yield: 6 servings | **Active time:** 15 minutes | **Start to finish:** 15 minutes

1½ pounds thick white-fleshed fish fillets
4 tablespoons (½ stick) unsalted butter
2 tablespoons olive oil
1 small onion, peeled and chopped
4 garlic cloves, peeled and minced
½ cup dry white wine
2 tablespoons lemon juice
¼ cup chopped fresh parsley
1 teaspoon Italian seasoning
Crushed red pepper flakes to taste

1. Rinse fish and pat dry with paper towels. Cut fish into 1-inch cubes and set aside.
2. Heat butter and oil in a large skillet over medium-high heat. When butter foam starts to subside, add onion and garlic, and cook, stirring frequently, for 3 minutes, or until onion is translucent. Add fish, and cook for 2 minutes, turning cubes gently with tongs.
3. Add wine, lemon juice, parsley, and Italian seasoning to the skillet. Stir well, and season to taste with red pepper flakes. Cook for 2 minutes. Serve immediately.

Note: The fish can be prepared for cooking up to 6 hours in advance and refrigerated, tightly covered.

Each serving contains:

....

65 MG SODIUM | 229 calories | 117 calories from fat | 13 g fat | 6 g saturated fat | 21 g protein | 3 g carbohydrates

Variation:

- Substitute boneless, skinless chicken breast halves, pounded to an even thickness of ½ inch between 2 sheets of plastic wrap and cut into 2-inch strips, for the fish. Cook the chicken for 3 minutes per side, or until the chicken is cooked through and no longer pink.

While butter gives food a delicious flavor, it should never be used alone when sautéing food. The reason is that all fats burn at a certain temperature, and the dairy solids in butter make that temperature rather low. That's why in recipes there is always some sort of oil added in to raise the smoke point.

Poached Marinated Mexican Fish

Because Southwestern cooking is an offshoot of the cuisine from land-locked Sonora province, we tend to forget that most of Mexico borders on either the Gulf of Mexico or the Pacific Ocean. This method of marinating fish prior to cooking comes from Veracruz. Serve the dish with some tortillas.

Yield: 6 servings | **Active time:** 20 minutes | **Start to finish:** 1½ hours, including 1 hour for marinating

   1½ pounds thick white-fleshed fish fillets
   2 (14.5-ounce) cans no-salt-added tomatoes, drained
   1 small onion, peeled and diced
   ¼ cup fresh cilantro leaves
   3 garlic cloves, peeled
   1 jalapeño or serrano chile, seeds and ribs removed
   ¼ cup lime juice
   ¼ cup olive oil, divided
   1 tablespoon smoked Spanish paprika
   2 teaspoons ground cumin
   1 teaspoon dried oregano
   ¼–½ teaspoon crushed red pepper flakes
   1 large green bell pepper, seeds and ribs removed, and thinly sliced
   1 medium red onion, peeled and thinly sliced
   ¾ cup Seafood Stock (recipe on page 29)

1. Rinse fish and pat dry with paper towels. Cut fish into 1-inch cubes and set aside.

2. Combine tomatoes, onion, cilantro, garlic, chile, and lime juice in a food processor fitted with the steel blade or in a blender. Puree until smooth, and scrape mixture into a heavy resealable plastic bag. Add 2 tablespoons oil, paprika, cumin, oregano, and red pepper flakes, and mix well. Add fish cubes and marinate fish, refrigerated, for 1 hour, turning the bag occasionally.

3. While fish marinates, heat remaining oil in a large skillet over medium-high heat. Add green bell pepper and red onion and cook, stirring frequently, for 3 minutes, or until onion is translucent. Add stock, reduce the heat to low, and simmer vegetables, covered, for 5 minutes.

4. Add fish and its marinade and bring to a boil. Cover the pan and cook fish for 3–5 minutes, or until fish is cooked through and flakes easily. Serve immediately.

Note: The dish can be prepared up to 1 day in advance and refrigerated, tightly covered. Reheat it over low heat, covered, stirring occasionally and gently, or serve it cold.

Each serving contains:

83 MG SODIUM | 207 calories | 77 calories from fat | 8.5 g fat | 1 g saturated fat | 22 g protein | 11 g carbohydrates

Cilantro, which is used extensively in both Hispanic and Asian cooking, is one food that people either love or hate. The best substitute is always flat-leaf Italian parsley.

Warm Fish, Avocado, and Grapefruit Salad

The pairing of two tropical ingredients—buttery avocado and tart grapefruit—has been popular for decades with good reason; it's delicious. In this salad the two fruits are joined with delicate fish fillets that absorb flavor from the mild and lean dressing.

Yield: 6 servings | **Active time:** 15 minutes | **Start to finish:** 25 minutes

1½ pounds thin white-fleshed fish fillets
1 tablespoon paprika
1 tablespoon chili powder
1 teaspoon ground cumin
1 teaspoon dried oregano
Freshly ground black pepper to taste
¼ cup grapefruit juice
2 tablespoons rice vinegar
2 garlic cloves, peeled and minced
⅔ cup olive oil, divided
2 pink grapefruits
6 cups bite-sized pieces romaine lettuce, rinsed and dried
4 scallions, white parts and 3 inches of green tops, rinsed, trimmed, and sliced
1 small cucumber, peeled, halved lengthwise, seeded, and sliced
1 ripe avocado, peeled and thinly sliced

1. Rinse fish and pat dry with paper towels. Cut fish into 2-inch squares. Combine paprika, chili powder, cumin, oregano, and pepper in a small bowl. Rub spice mixture on both sides of fillets.
2. Combine grapefruit juice, vinegar, garlic, and pepper in a jar with a tight-fitting lid, and shake well. Add ⅓ cup olive oil, and shake well again. Set aside.
3. Peel grapefruit, and cut off white pith. Cut grapefruit into thin slices, discarding seeds if necessary. Arrange grapefruit on individual plates or on a serving platter. Top grapefruit with lettuce and divide scallions, cucumber, and avocado on top.
4. Heat remaining oil in a large skillet over medium-high heat. Cook fish for 2 minutes per side, turning it gently with a slotted spatula. Remove fish from the skillet and drain on paper towels. Arrange fish on top of salad and drizzle all with dressing. Serve immediately.

Note: The fish can also be cooked up to 1 day in advance and refrigerated, tightly covered, and the dressing can be prepared at the same time. Serve the fish cold; do not reheat.

Each serving contains:

83 MG SODIUM | 347 calories | 189 calories from fat | 21 g fat | 3 g saturated fat | 23 g protein | 19 g carbohydrates

Variation:
- Substitute boneless, skinless chicken breast halves, pounded between 2 sheets of plastic wrap to an even thickness of $\frac{1}{4}$ inch, for the fish. Cook chicken for 2–3 minutes per side, or until chicken is cooked through and no longer pink.

You should always add granular seasonings like sugar to a salad dressing before adding the oil. These ingredients dissolve in liquid but not in oil.

Mediterranean Tuna and Pasta Salad

Lots of fresh, crunchy vegetables are in every bite of this refreshing salad tossed with pasta in a lemony dressing. It's a full meal with nothing else needed.

Yield: 6 servings | **Active time:** 15 minutes | **Start to finish:** 25 minutes

½ pound green beans, rinsed, trimmed, and cut into 1-inch lengths
⅔ pound small pasta shells or gemelli
4 (4.5-ounce) cans low-sodium light tuna
⅓ cup lemon juice
1 tablespoon Marvelous Mustard (recipe on page 40)
1 tablespoon chopped fresh parsley
1 teaspoon herbes de Provence
2 garlic cloves, peeled and minced
Freshly ground black pepper to taste
½ cup olive oil
½ green bell pepper, seeds and ribs removed, and diced
½ small red onion, peeled and diced
½ small fennel bulb, rinsed, trimmed, and diced
3 ripe plum tomatoes, rinsed, cored, seeded, and chopped
3 cups bite-sized pieces salad greens, rinsed and dried
2 hard-cooked eggs, cut into wedges (optional)

1. Bring a pot of salted water to a boil, and have a bowl of ice water handy. Boil green beans for 2–3 minutes, or until crisp-tender. Remove beans from the water with a slotted spoon, and plunge them into the ice water to stop the cooking action. Drain when chilled, and place beans in a large mixing bowl.

2. Add pasta to the boiling water and cook according to package directions until al dente. Drain and run under cold water until cold. Add pasta and tuna to the mixing bowl.

3. Combine lemon juice, mustard, parsley, herbes de Provence, garlic, and pepper in a jar with a tight-fitting lid, and shake well. Add olive oil, and shake well again.

4. Add dressing to the mixing bowl, and allow to sit for 5 minutes so pasta absorbs flavor. Add green bell pepper, onion, fennel, and tomatoes, and toss. To serve, arrange lettuce on individual plates or on a serving platter, and top with salad. Serve immediately, garnished with egg wedges, if using.

Note: The salad can be prepared up to 1 day in advance and refrigerated, tightly covered. Allow it to sit at room temperature for 30 minutes prior to serving.

Each serving contains:

167 MG SODIUM | 539 calories | 148 calories from fat | 16.5 g fat | 2 g saturated fat | 30 g protein | 71 g carbohydrates

Variation:
- Substitute 1½ cups diced cooked chicken for the tuna.

Running pasta under cold water after draining speeds up the completion of all pasta salads. It's not as effective to soak it in cold water because the pasta has a tendency to become soggy.

Chapter 7:
Poultry Prowess

The tiny chicken has passed the huge cow in popularity, and a good part of that popularity is due to its relatively low cost. There's no such thing as a cut of beef for less than $1 a pound, but you can buy a whole chicken for that cost even with today's skyrocketing food costs. If you're like most Americans, there's some sort of poultry in the center of your dinner plate about three times a week.

The delicate flavor of chicken makes it a candidate for countless ways of seasoning, and the fact that it's relatively quick to cook means that chicken is consistent with today's busy lifestyle. But this delicacy is a two-edged sword when following a low-sodium diet. It takes a lot of extra seasoning and ingredients to produce a vibrantly flavored dish. Those are the recipes you'll find in this chapter.

The majority of the recipes are for whole chickens that have been cut up, but then there are other recipes for the coveted boneless, skinless breasts because those are frequently put on sale as "loss leaders" at supermarkets; that's the time to stock up on them.

While this is a rather extensive chapter, you'll find a whole book of recipes for this versatile bird in *$3 Chicken Meals*.

CHOOSING THE CHOICEST

Look for packages of chicken that do not have an accumulation of liquid in the bottom. That can be a sign that the chicken has been frozen and thawed. Chicken should be stored in the coldest part of the refrigerator (40°F or below), sealed as it comes from the market and used within two or three days.

If it should be necessary to keep it longer, freeze it. While freezing can reduce flavor, moisture, and tenderness, it will preserve freshness. Seal poultry in an airtight container, heavy plastic bag, plastic wrap, foil, or freezer paper. Label the package with the date on which it was frozen. Uncooked poultry can be stored frozen up to six months; cooked poultry should be used within three months.

To defrost, place the frozen chicken on a plate in the refrigerator or use the microwave, following manufacturer's instructions. To speed the thawing of uncooked chicken, place package in cold water, changing the water frequently.

Chicken should be rinsed under cold running water when it is removed from the wrapper, and have absolutely no aroma. If it has any off smells, take it back to the supermarket if it's before the expiration date, or discard it if it's after that date or you took it out of the freezer.

Illness-causing bacteria such as salmonella can grow in high-protein, low acid foods like poultry, so special handling should always be taken with raw chicken or turkey. To prevent transferring bacteria from one food to another, use warm water and soap to wash your hands, cooking utensils, and work surfaces before and after use. Here are some common foibles when handling chicken:

- **Never put cooked chicken on the same platter that held it raw.** Hospital emergency rooms see many cases of food poisoning in summer because of this. If you transport marinated chicken pieces outside to a grill, bring in the platter and wash it well before placing the cooked chicken on it.

- **Never refrigerate raw chicken with any other foods.** If you want to prep the ingredients for a chicken dish in advance, keep the chicken in a separate plastic bag from the other ingredients. And cut up the chicken last so there's no chance that your vegetables were exposed to bacteria on the cutting board.

- **Never partially cook chicken.** I have been horrified over the years to hear about people partially cooking chicken in the oven and then putting it on the grill a few hours later. Chicken must pass through the "danger zone" of 40°F to 140°F as quickly as possible.

CUNNINGLY CUTTING

Just look at the range of prices for chicken in the supermarket! They can range from less than $1 per pound for whole birds and leg/thigh quarters to $5 or $6 per pound for coveted boneless, skinless breasts. Always keep in mind that you're paying for someone else's labor.

It is far more economical to purchase a whole chicken, and cut it up yourself, rather than buying one already cut. Another benefit is that you can save the scraps and freeze them to keep you "stocked up" for soups and sauces. Here are some methods of chicken cutting you should know:

- Cutting up a whole chicken: Start by breaking back the wings until the joints snap Then use a boning knife to cut through the ball joints and detach the wings; cut off the wing tips and save them for stock. When holding the chicken on its side, you will see a natural curve outlining the boundary between the breast and the leg/thigh quarters. Use sharp kitchen shears and cut along this line. Cut the breast in half by scraping away the meat from the breastbone and using a small paring knife to remove the wishbone. Cut away the breastbone using the shears and save it for stock. Divide the leg/thigh quarters by turning the pieces over and finding the joint joining them. Cut through the joint and sever the leg from the thigh.

- Boning chicken breasts: If possible, buy the chicken breasts whole rather than split. Pull the skin off with your fingers, and then make an incision on either side of the breastbone, cutting down until you feel the bone resisting the knife. Treating one side at a time, place the blade of your boning knife against the carcass and scrape away the meat. You will then have two pieces—the large fillet and the small tenderloin. To trim the fillet, cut away any fat. Some recipes will tell you to pound the breast to an even thickness so it will cook evenly and quickly. Place the breast between 2 sheets of plastic wrap or waxed paper and pound with the smooth side of a meat mallet or the bottom of a small, heavy skillet or saucepan. If you have a favorite veal scallop recipe and want to substitute chicken or turkey, pound it very thin—to a thickness of $1/4$ inch. Otherwise, your goal is to pound the thicker portion so that it lies flat and cooks evenly. To trim the tenderloin, secure the tip of the tendon that will be visible with your free hand. Using a paring knife, scrape down the tendon, and the meat will push away.

COOKING CHICKEN CORRECTLY

The rules have changed for cooking poultry in the last year, and the revision means that you can avoid overcooked, dry chicken and turkey. The minimum temperature is now 165°F for both white and dark meat. At that temperature there's no chance for microorganisms to survive.

The best way to test this is to use an instant-read meat thermometer. When the thickest part of the chicken is probed, the reading should be 165°F. If you do not want to take the temperature of every piece of chicken, recognize these visual signals: the chicken should be tender when poked with the tip of a paring knife, there should not be a hint of pink even near the bones, and the juices should run clear. Always test the dark meat before the white meat. Dark meat takes slightly longer to cook, so if the thighs are the proper temperature, you know the breasts will be fine.

CUTTING THE CALORIES

If you say "wow" at the number of calories contained in some of these chicken recipes, it's because the recipes were calculated with the assumption that you're going to eat the chicken skin, which is where more than half the fat on a chicken is located.

According to the U.S. Department of Agriculture, it makes no difference in the fat content if the skin is discarded before or after the chicken is cooked. From the culinary perspective, chicken remains far moister and more tender if cooked with the skin. The exceptions are recipes formulated for quick-cooking boneless, skinless breasts and thighs.

It's also easier to discard the skin after the chicken is cooked. So cook the chicken pieces or whole chicken with the skin attached, and then decide after it is cooked if you want to enjoy the crispy skin or save those calories and discard it.

Italian Chicken with Mushrooms

This dish is a version of chicken cacciatore. It's subtly seasoned, and sauces the chicken with tomatoes and lots of herbs. Serve the sauce over some whole-wheat pasta or brown rice.

Yield: 6 servings | **Active time:** 20 minutes | **Start to finish:** 55 minutes

¼ cup dried mushrooms, such as porcini
½ cup boiling water
6 (6-ounce) skinless chicken breasts, with bones
3 tablespoons olive oil
1 medium onion, peeled and diced
3 garlic cloves, peeled and minced
1 green bell pepper, seeds and ribs removed, and diced
¾ pound fresh mushrooms, wiped with a damp paper towel, trimmed, and sliced
½ cup dry white wine
1 (14.5-ounce) can no-salt-added diced tomatoes, undrained
1 (8-ounce) can no-salt-added tomato sauce
3 tablespoons chopped fresh parsley
1 tablespoon Italian seasoning
Freshly ground black pepper to taste

1. Preheat the oven broiler, and line a broiler pan with heavy-duty aluminum foil. Combine dried mushrooms and boiling water, pushing them down into the water. Soak for 10 minutes, then drain mushrooms, reserving soaking liquid, and chop mushrooms. Strain soaking liquid through a sieve lined with a paper coffee filter or a paper towel. Set aside.

2. Rinse chicken and pat dry with paper towels. Broil chicken pieces for 3–5 minutes per side, or until browned. Transfer chicken to a roasting pan, bone side up, and preheat the oven to 375°F.

3. While chicken browns, heat oil in a large skillet over medium-high heat, swirling to coat the pan. Add onion, garlic, green bell pepper, and fresh mushrooms. Cook, stirring frequently, for 5–7 minutes, or until mushrooms soften. Add dried mushrooms, mushroom soaking liquid, wine, tomatoes, tomato sauce, parsley, and Italian seasoning. Bring to a boil over medium-high heat, stirring occasionally.

4. Pour sauce over chicken in the roasting pan. Bake chicken, covered, for 30–40 minutes, or until chicken is cooked through and no longer pink and an instant-read thermometer registers 165°F.
5. Remove chicken from the pan with tongs and keep warm. Place the roasting pan on the stove and reduce sauce by ¼ over high heat, stirring frequently. Season to taste with pepper, and serve immediately.

Note: The chicken can be cooked up to 2 days in advance and refrigerated, tightly covered. Reheat it, covered, in a 350°F oven for 20–25 minutes, or until hot.

Each serving contains:

149 MG SODIUM | 287 calories | 42 calories from fat | 5 g fat | 1 g saturated fat | 43 g protein | 16 g carbohydrates

Variation:
- Substitute thick white-fleshed fish fillets for the chicken. They do not need to be browned, and should be added to the sauce and baked for 10–15 minutes, or until the fish is cooked through and flakes easily.

While dried wild mushrooms are quite expensive, you never use very many of them and they add incredible flavor and aroma to dishes. It is important, however, to strain the liquid because it is frequently filled with grit.

Chicken Marsala

Now here's a healthy dish that's on the table in less time than it takes to get that sky-high-sodium pizza delivered! The sauce is lean, but contains lots of garlic as well as heady Marsala wine; serve the sauce over some whole-wheat pasta or brown rice.

Yield: 6 servings | **Active time:** 15 minutes | **Start to finish:** 25 minutes

1½ pounds boneless, skinless chicken breast halves
3 tablespoons all-purpose flour
Freshly ground black pepper to taste
¼ cup olive oil, divided
1 small onion, peeled and diced
6–8 garlic cloves, peeled and minced
1 pound mushrooms, wiped with a damp paper towel, trimmed, and thinly sliced
1 cup dry Marsala wine
¾ cup Chicken Stock (recipe on page 26)
⅓ cup chopped fresh parsley
1½ teaspoons Italian seasoning

1. Rinse chicken and pat dry with paper towels. Trim chicken of all visible fat, and cut into 1-inch cubes. Season flour to taste with pepper. Dust chicken with seasoned flour, shaking off any excess.
2. Heat 2 tablespoons oil in a large skillet over medium-high heat, swirling to coat the pan. Add chicken pieces and cook, stirring frequently, for 3 minutes, or until chicken is opaque. Remove chicken from the pan with a slotted spoon and set aside.
3. Add remaining oil, and then add onion, garlic, and mushrooms to the skillet. Cook, stirring frequently, for 3 minutes, or until onion is translucent. Return chicken to the skillet and add Marsala, stock, parsley, and Italian seasoning. Bring to a boil, stirring occasionally.
4. Reduce the heat to medium and simmer mixture, uncovered, for 10–15 minutes, or until chicken is cooked through and no longer pink. Season to taste with pepper. Serve immediately.

Note: The dish can be prepared up to 1 day in advance and refrigerated, tightly covered. Reheat it over low heat, covered, until hot.

Each serving contains:

349 MG SODIUM | 231 calories | 75 calories from fat | 8 g fat | 2 g satu-
rated fat | 27 g protein | 12 g carbohydrates

Variation:
- Substitute boneless pork loin, cut into thin strips, for the chicken.

> Marsala is a fortified wine similar in many regards to sherry and port. Originally the alcohol was added to allow the wine to survive long ocean voyages, and it became very popular in England during the eighteenth century.

Tandoori Chicken

This healthful Indian dish is briefly marinated in seasoned yogurt, which tenderizes the chicken as well as flavoring it. In India it is cooked in a steep-sided tandoor oven, but an all-American grill or oven broiler also does the trick. For a wrap sandwich, use *nan* or a whole-wheat tortilla.

Yield: 6 servings | **Active time:** 15 minutes | **Start to finish:** 1½ hours, including 1 hour to marinate

6 (8-inch) bamboo skewers
1¼ pounds boneless, skinless chicken breast halves
¾ cup plain nonfat yogurt
2 tablespoons lemon juice
3 garlic cloves, peeled and pressed through a garlic press
1 tablespoon grated fresh ginger
1 tablespoon ground turmeric
2 teaspoons ground coriander
1 teaspoon ground cumin
Cayenne to taste
Vegetable oil spray

1. Soak bamboo skewers in water to cover.
2. Rinse chicken and pat dry with paper towels. Trim chicken breasts of all visible fat, and cut into 1-inch cubes. Combine yogurt, lemon juice, garlic, ginger, turmeric, coriander, cumin, and cayenne in a heavy resealable plastic bag. Add chicken, and marinate at room temperature for 1 hour or up to 4 hours refrigerated, turning the bag occasionally.
3. Light a charcoal or gas grill, or preheat the oven broiler. Remove chicken from marinade and discard marinade. Thread chicken onto bamboo skewers and spray chicken with vegetable oil.
4. Grill chicken for 3–4 minutes per side, uncovered and turning it in quarter turns with tongs, or until chicken is cooked through and no longer pink. Serve immediately.

Note: The marinade can be prepared up to 1 day in advance and refrigerated, tightly covered.

Each serving contains:

72.5 MG SODIUM | 118 calories | 12 calories from fat | 1 g fat | 0 g saturated fat | 23 g protein | 2 g carbohydrates

Variation:

- Substitute thick white-fleshed fish fillets for the chicken. They will cook in the same amount of time.

Any food described as "tandoori" gets its name from the traditional Indian tandoor oven in which it's cooked. The tandoor is a round oven with glowing coals at the bottom. Traditionally meat is skewered and suspended over the hot coals, and nan breads are baked on the walls of the oven. Most food cooked in a tandoor oven is first marinated to give it moisture after it's subjected to the high-heat cooking process.

Grilled Turkey Ensalata

This is the poultry version of a classic Italian dish traditionally made with veal, in which the meat is topped with essentially a tossed salad. It is incredibly refreshing on a hot summer day, and the vinegar in the salad enlivens the flavor of the turkey, too.

Yield: 6 servings | **Active time:** 20 minutes | **Start to finish:** 30 minutes

Vegetable oil spray
1½ pounds sliced turkey cutlets
2 teaspoons Italian seasoning
Freshly ground black pepper to taste
¼ cup balsamic vinegar
3 garlic cloves, peeled and minced
2 tablespoons chopped fresh parsley
1 teaspoon dried oregano
½ teaspoon dried thyme
⅓ cup olive oil
6 ripe plum tomatoes, rinsed, cored, seeded, and chopped
1½ cups finely chopped iceberg lettuce
4 scallions, white parts and 3 inches of green tops, rinsed, trimmed, and chopped

1. Light a charcoal or gas grill, or preheat the oven broiler. Spray turkey with vegetable oil spray, and sprinkle with Italian seasoning and pepper. Set aside.

2. Combine vinegar, garlic, parsley, oregano, thyme, and pepper in a jar with a tight-fitting lid, and shake well. Add olive oil, and shake well again. Set aside.

3. Grill turkey for 2–3 minutes per side, uncovered, or until cooked through and no longer pink. Remove turkey from the grill, and keep warm.

4. Combine tomatoes, lettuce, and scallions in a mixing bowl. Toss with dressing, and season to taste with pepper. To serve, top each cutlet with a portion of salad mixture and serve immediately.

Note: The dressing can be prepared up to 1 day in advance and refrigerated, tightly covered. Allow it to reach room temperature before using.

Each serving contains:

87 MG SODIUM | 241 calories | 97 calories from fat | 11 g fat | 2 g saturated fat | 27.5 g protein | 9 g carbohydrates

Variation:
- Substitute boneless pork loin, cut into ½-inch-thick slices, for the turkey.

Balsamic vinegar hails from Modena, a city also known for its production of Parmesan cheese. True balsamic vinegar is made from a reduction of syrup from sweet wine grapes, which is then aged for a minimum of twelve years.

Chicken with Chutney

Chutney is a wonderful low-sodium sauce for foods; its sweet-sour-spicy eating profile and range of succulent ingredients work with a variety of foods—including these chicken thighs. Serve this with a steamed green vegetable and some brown rice braised in stock.

Yield: 6 servings | **Active time:** 20 minutes | **Start to finish:** 50 minutes

    12 boneless, skinless chicken thighs
    Freshly ground black pepper to taste
    1 tablespoon vegetable oil
    1 small onion, peeled and diced
    3 garlic cloves, peeled and minced
    1 Golden Delicious apple, cored and chopped
    1 (14.5-ounce) can diced no-salt-added tomatoes, undrained
    $\frac{1}{4}$ cup chopped dried apricots
    2 tablespoons raisins
    2 tablespoons cider vinegar
    2 tablespoons firmly packed dark brown sugar
    $\frac{1}{4}$–$\frac{1}{2}$ teaspoon crushed red pepper flakes, or to taste
    3 cups cooked brown rice, hot

1. Preheat the oven to 350°F, and line a 9 x 13-inch baking pan with aluminum foil. Rinse chicken and pat dry with paper towels. Sprinkle chicken with pepper, and arrange chicken in the baking pan.

2. Heat oil in a large skillet over medium-high heat, swirling to coat the pan. Add onion and garlic, and cook, stirring frequently, for 3 minutes, or until onion is translucent. Add apple, tomatoes, apricots, raisins, vinegar, brown sugar, and crushed red pepper flakes to the skillet. Cook, stirring frequently, for 5–7 minutes, or until vegetables are soft and mixture has slightly thickened. Season to taste with pepper.

3. Pour sauce over chicken and bake, covered with foil, for 30–40 minutes, or until chicken is cooked through and no longer pink and registers 165°F on an instant-read thermometer. Serve immediately over rice.

Note: The dish can be prepared up to 2 days in advance and refrigerated, tightly covered. Reheat it, covered, in a 350°F oven for 20–25 minutes, or until hot. It is also excellent served cold.

Each serving contains:

147 MG SODIUM | 247 calories | 65 calories from fat | 7 g fat | 2 g satu-
rated fat | 28 g protein | 17 g carbohydrates

Variation:

- Substitute boneless pork loin, cut into $\frac{1}{2}$-inch-thick slices, for the chicken. Brown pork in the skillet, and decrease baking time to 15 minutes.

While there are numerous varieties of apples available, the Golden Delicious is my favorite for cooking. It has some natural sweetness and retains its texture when cooked. The Granny Smith is an alternative, but it is not as sweet and will require more sugar if using it as a substitute.

French Lemon and Roasted Garlic Chicken

This easy baked dish is actually a variation on the traditional Chicken with Forty Cloves of Garlic. But don't be afraid of the garlic; it becomes mellow and sweet when it's cooked in this way. The lemon juice perks the palate and takes the place of salt in seasoning the dish.

Yield: 6 servings | **Active time:** 15 minutes | **Start to finish:** 40 minutes

1 (3½–4-pound) frying chicken, cut into serving pieces, with each breast half cut crosswise in half
Freshly ground black pepper to taste
2 teaspoons dried thyme
¼ cup olive oil
2 heads garlic, broken into cloves but not peeled
1 cup Chicken Stock (recipe on page 26)
¼ cup lemon juice
2 tablespoons chopped fresh parsley

1. Preheat the oven to 400°F, and grease a 10 x 14-inch baking pan. Rinse chicken and pat dry with paper towels. Sprinkle chicken with pepper and rub with thyme.
2. Heat oil in a large skillet over medium-high heat. Brown chicken for 2 minutes per side, or until browned, turning chicken with tongs. Remove chicken from the skillet and transfer it to the prepared pan with the skin side up.
3. Add garlic cloves to the skillet and brown for 2 minutes. Add stock and lemon juice to the skillet, and bring to a boil. Pour mixture over chicken.
4. Bake chicken for 25 minutes, or until chicken is cooked through and no longer pink and an instant-read thermometer registers 165°F when inserted into the thigh. Season to taste with pepper and serve immediately, sprinkling each serving with parsley.

Note: The dish can be cooked up to 2 days in advance and refrigerated, tightly covered. Reheat in a 350°F oven, covered, for 20–25 minutes, or until hot.

Each serving contains:

190 MG SODIUM | 620 calories | 399 calories from fat | 44 g fat | 12 g saturated fat | 50 g protein | 3 g carbohydrates

Variations:
- Substitute lime juice for the lemon juice.
- Substitute bone-in pork chops for the chicken, and cook them for a total of 30 minutes.

I usually throw in an extra head or two of garlic when making this dish. That way I can peel and puree the extra cloves to use in mashed potatoes or spread on crostini. Remove the additional garlic before adding the stock and lemon juice.

Apricot Mustard Chicken

Succulent dried apricots and sharp mustard combine to give this low-sodium dish a sophisticated and dynamic sweet and sour flavor. Serve the sauce over some buttered egg noodles with a tossed salad on the side.

Yield: 6 servings | **Active time:** 20 minutes | **Start to finish:** 50 minutes

> 1 (3½–4-pound) frying chicken, cut into serving pieces, with each
>   breast half cut crosswise in half
> Freshly ground black pepper to taste
> ½ cup all-purpose flour, divided
> 3 tablespoons unsalted butter
> 2 tablespoons olive oil
> 1½ cups Chicken Stock (recipe on page 26)
> ½ cup dry white wine
> ¾ cup chopped dried apricots
> 2 tablespoons firmly packed dark brown sugar
> 1 tablespoon mustard powder

1. Rinse chicken and pat dry with paper towels. Sprinkle chicken with pepper. Reserve 2 tablespoons flour, and place remaining flour on a sheet of plastic wrap.
2. Heat butter and oil in a large, covered skillet over medium-high heat. Dredge chicken in flour, shaking off any excess. Brown chicken for 2–3 minutes per side, or until browned, turning chicken with tongs. Remove chicken from the skillet, and set aside.
3. Reduce the heat to low, stir in reserved flour, and cook for 1 minute, stirring constantly. Whisk in stock, wine, dried apricots, brown sugar, and mustard powder, and bring to a boil over medium-high heat.
4. Return chicken to the skillet, reduce the heat to low, and cook chicken, covered, for 25–30 minutes, or until chicken is cooked through and no longer pink, and an instant-read thermometer registers 165°F when inserted into the thigh. Season to taste with pepper, and serve immediately.

Note: The dish can be cooked up to 2 days in advance and refrigerated, tightly covered. Reheat it in a 350°F oven, covered, for 20–25 minutes, or until hot.

Each serving contains:

281 MG SODIUM | 732 calories | 428 calories from fat | 47.5 g fat | 15 g saturated fat | 51 g protein | 21 g carbohydrates

Variation:
- Substitute 3 fresh peaches, peeled and cut into ¾-inch dice, for the dried apricots. Add the peaches after the chicken has cooked for 15 minutes.

Tongs are one of the most important utensils you can have in a kitchen. They make it possible to turn food without puncturing it, which allows juices to escape. Use tongs for any recipe dealing with whole chicken pieces and also when turning any food on the grill.

Greek Baked Chicken

Garlic, lemon, and oregano are all hallmarks of Greek cooking, and they are the dominant flavors in this one-dish meal that also includes cubes of potato as well as carrots and mushrooms. The seasonings permeate the potato so that it doesn't taste bland without salt.

Yield: 6 servings | **Active time:** 15 minutes | **Start to finish:** 1½ hours

> 1 (3½–4-pound) frying chicken, cut into serving pieces, with each breast half cut crosswise in half
> 3 large baking potatoes, peeled and cut into 1½-inch chunks
> 2 carrots, peeled and cut into 1½-inch chunks
> ¼ pound mushrooms, wiped with a damp paper towel, trimmed, and halved if large
> 1 cup Chicken Stock (recipe on page 26)
> ½ cup lemon juice
> ½ cup dry white wine
> ¼ cup olive oil
> 6 garlic cloves, peeled and minced
> 1½ tablespoons dried oregano
> Freshly ground black pepper to taste

1. Preheat the oven to 375°F, and line a 10 x 14-inch baking pan with heavy-duty aluminum foil.
2. Arrange chicken, potatoes, carrots, and mushrooms in the prepared pan, with chicken pieces skin side down. Combine stock, lemon juice, wine, oil, garlic, oregano, and pepper in a jar with a tight-fitting lid, and shake well. Pour mixture over chicken and vegetables.
3. Bake, uncovered, for 30 minutes. Remove the pan from the oven and turn over chicken pieces and vegetables with tongs. Bake for an additional 45–55 minutes, or until vegetables are tender and chicken is cooked through and no longer pink and registers 165°F on an instant-read thermometer.

Note: The dish can be cooked up to 2 days in advance and refrigerated, tightly covered. Reheat it in a 350°F oven, covered, for 20–25 minutes, or until hot.

Each serving contains:

208 MG SODIUM | 690 calories | 385 calories from fat | 43 g fat | 12 g saturated fat | 52 g protein | 21 g carbohydrates

Spicy Caribbean Chicken Wings

These spicy wings are marinated in what's commonly called "jerk seasoning."

Yield: 6 servings | **Active time:** 15 minutes | **Start to finish:** 7 hours, including 6 hours for marinating

18 chicken wings, separated into 2 pieces with wing tips reserved
   for making stock
1/3 cup olive oil
2 tablespoons soy sauce
1 small onion, peeled and diced
3 garlic cloves, peeled
2 jalapeño or serrano chiles, seeds and ribs removed, and diced
1 teaspoon ground allspice
1 teaspoon dried thyme
1/2 teaspoon ground cinnamon
1/2 teaspoon ground nutmeg
Freshly ground black pepper to taste

1. Rinse wings and pat dry with paper towels. Place wings in a heavy resealable plastic bag. Combine olive oil, soy sauce, onion, garlic, chiles, allspice, thyme, cinnamon, nutmeg, and pepper in a food processor fitted with the steel blade or in a blender. Puree until smooth. Add marinade to the bag with wings.
2. Marinate chicken wings, refrigerated, for at least 6 hours, preferably overnight, turning the bag occasionally.
3. Preheat the oven to 425°F, and line 2 baking sheets with heavy-duty aluminum foil.
4. Remove wings from marinade and discard marinade. Arrange wings in a single layer on the baking sheet. Bake wings for 35–40 minutes, turning them with tongs after 20 minutes, or until wings are cooked through and no longer pink. Serve wings hot, at room temperature, or chilled.

Note: The wings can be cooked up to 2 days in advance and refrigerated, tightly covered. Serve them cold, or reheat them, uncovered, in a 350°F oven for 12–15 minutes, or until hot.

Each serving contains:

108 MG SODIUM | 373 calories | 252 calories from fat | 28 g fat | 7 g saturated fat | 27 g protein | 1.5 g carbohydrates

Grilled North African Chicken

North African cooking is characterized by a combination of flavorful and aromatic spices such as the cumin, cinnamon, and coriander in this recipe. Serve the sauce over some couscous, and place a crunchy tossed salad alongside.

Yield: 6 servings | **Active time:** 20 minutes | **Start to finish:** 5 hours, including 4 hours for marinating

> 1 (3½–4-pound) frying chicken, cut into serving pieces, with each breast half cut crosswise in half
> ¼ cup red wine vinegar
> ½ small onion, peeled and chopped
> 3 garlic cloves, peeled and minced
> 3 tablespoons ground cumin
> 2 tablespoons ground coriander
> 1 tablespoon firmly packed dark brown sugar
> 1 teaspoon ground cinnamon
> Cayenne to taste
> ⅔ cup olive oil
> ¼ cup chopped fresh cilantro

1. Rinse chicken and pat dry with paper towels. Combine vinegar, onion, garlic, cumin, coriander, brown sugar, cinnamon, and cayenne in a heavy resealable plastic bag, and mix well. Add oil, and mix well again. Add chicken pieces, and marinate chicken, refrigerated, for a minimum of 4 hours and up to 12 hours, turning the bag occasionally.
2. Light a charcoal or gas grill, or preheat the oven broiler.
3. Remove chicken from marinade, and transfer marinade to a small saucepan. Grill chicken, covered, starting with skin side down, for 8–10 minutes per side, or until chicken is cooked through and no longer pink and dark meat registers 165°F on an instant-read thermometer.
4. Remove as much oil as possible from the top of marinade with a soup ladle. Bring marinade to a boil over medium-high heat, stirring occasionally. Reduce the heat to low, and simmer for 5 minutes. Remove chicken from the grill, and serve immediately, sprinkled with cilantro and passing sauce separately.

Note: The chicken can be grilled up to 1 day in advance and refrigerated, tightly covered. Serve it cold, or reheat it in a 350°F oven for 12–15 minutes, or until hot.

Each serving contains:

188 MG SODIUM | 645 calories | 420 calories from fat | 47 g fat | 12 g saturated fat | 49 g protein | 4 g carbohydrates

Variation:
- Substitute 1½ pounds boneless pork loin, cut into ¾-inch slices, for the chicken. Grill pork for 4–5 minutes per side, or to desired doneness.

If a marinade is to be used as a sauce once food is cooked, it must be simmered for a few minutes to ensure that any bacteria that may have been transferred from the raw food are eliminated.

Mexican Chicken with Molé Sauce

Molé, pronounced *MOH-lay,* is an ancient Mexican spicy sauce that dates from the Aztec era. Adding to its richness is unsweetened chocolate, and it always includes some sort of nut or legume for thickening. Serve this chicken with rice to enjoy the sauce.

Yield: 6 servings | **Active time:** 15 minutes | **Start to finish:** 55 minutes

1 (3½–4-pound) frying chicken, cut into serving pieces, with each breast half cut crosswise in half
5 tablespoons olive oil, divided
6 garlic cloves, peeled and minced, divided
4 tablespoons chili powder, divided
Cayenne to taste
2 medium onions, peeled and chopped
2 teaspoons ground cumin
2 cups Chicken Stock (recipe on page 26)
1 (14.5-ounce) can no-salt-added diced tomatoes, drained
¼ cup peanut butter
¼ cup chopped raisins
1 tablespoon granulated sugar
1 tablespoon unsweetened cocoa powder (not Dutch processed)
3 cups cooked brown or white rice, hot

1. Preheat the oven to 350°F, and line a low baking pan with heavy-duty aluminum foil.

2. Rinse chicken and pat dry with paper towels. Combine 3 tablespoons oil, 2 garlic cloves, and 2 tablespoons chili powder in a small bowl. Season to taste with cayenne. Mix well, and rub mixture on chicken. Arrange chicken on the prepared pan, skin side down.

3. Bake chicken for 20 minutes, then turn with tongs, and bake skin side up for an additional 20–25 minutes, or until chicken is cooked through and no longer pink and registers 165°F on an instant-read thermometer.

4. While chicken bakes, make sauce. Heat remaining 2 tablespoons oil in a heavy saucepan over medium-high heat. Add onions and remaining garlic and cook, stirring frequently, for 3 minutes, or until onions are translucent. Stir in remaining chili powder and cumin and cook for 1 minute, stirring constantly.

5. Add stock, tomatoes, peanut butter, raisins, sugar, and cocoa powder. Stir well, and bring to a boil over high heat. Reduce the heat to low, and simmer sauce, uncovered, for 15 minutes, or until lightly thickened. Season to taste with cayenne. Serve sauce on top of chicken.

Note: The sauce can be prepared up to 2 days in advance and refrigerated, tightly covered. Reheat over low heat, stirring occasionally. The sauce can also be frozen for up to 3 months.

Each serving contains:

303 MG SODIUM | 714 calories | 427 calories from fat | 47.5 g fat | 13 g saturated fat | 53 g protein | 19 g carbohydrates

Variation:
- Substitute grilled or baked pork chops for the chicken.

Hickory-Smoked Beer Can Chicken

There is almost a cult following for this method of cooking a whole chicken, and until I tried it a few years ago, I was skeptical. But it does create a tender and moist chicken, and using wood chips on the grill adds flavor without sodium.

Yield: 4 servings | **Active time:** 10 minutes | **Start to finish:** 2 hours

>   2 cups hickory chips
>   (3–3½-pound) whole chicken
>   ¼ cup Creole Rub (recipe on page 41)
>   1 (12-ounce) can beer

1. Light a charcoal or gas grill, and arrange it for indirect cooking. If using a charcoal grill, soak hickory chips in water for 30 minutes. If using a gas grill, create a packet for the wood chips using heavy-duty aluminum foil and poke holes in the foil.

2. Rinse chicken and pat dry with paper towels, and remove giblets, if necessary. Save wing tips and giblets for making Chicken Stock (recipe on page 26); freeze liver separately. Rub 1 tablespoon Creole Rub inside cavity of chicken, rub 1 tablespoon under skin of breast meat, and rub 1 tablespoon over skin of chicken.

3. Pop top on the beer can, and pour off top 1 inch of beer. Use the pointed side of a bottle opener to punch 6 holes in the top of the beer can. Spoon remaining 1 tablespoon seasoning mixture through holes into beer.

4. Place an aluminum foil pan in the center of the grill grate, and add drained wood chips to coals if using a charcoal grill or place packet on burners if using a gas grill. Replace top grate. Holding chicken vertically, with the opening to the body cavity down, insert the beer can into the cavity. Stand chicken up in the center of the top grate, pulling out the legs to form a stable tripod with the beer can.

5. Grill chicken for 1½–2 hours, or until dark meat registers 165°F on an instant-read thermometer. If using a charcoal grill, add 10–15 fresh coals per side to the fire after 1 hour. Using tongs, lift chicken onto a platter, holding a spatula under the beer can. Allow chicken to rest for 10 minutes, then remove it from the beer can and carve. Serve immediately.

Note: The chicken can be grilled up to 1 day in advance and refrigerated, tightly covered. Serve it cold, or reheat it in a 350°F oven for 20-25 minutes, or until hot.

Each serving contains:

236.5 MG SODIUM | 788 calories | 54 calories from fat | 54 g fat | 15.5 g saturated fat | 59.5 g protein | 6 g carbohydrates

Variations:
- Substitute any of the spice rubs in Chapter 2 for the Creole Rub.
- Substitute white wine for the beer, and pour it into an empty soft drink or beer can.
- Substitute mesquite or apple wood chips for the hickory.

Beer can holders are now sold for less than $1 in many stores. If you like making chicken this way it's worth the investment because it adds stability to the chicken on the grill.

Black Bean Turkey Chili

Black beans may not be traditional in chili, but I like their earthiness more than that of pinto beans. There's a bit of wine in this recipe, too, which adds depth of flavor. Serve it over rice, with a tossed salad on the side.

Yield: 6 servings | **Active time:** 15 minutes | **Start to finish:** 1 hour

2 tablespoons olive oil

1 medium onion, peeled and diced

1 green bell pepper, seeds and ribs removed, and diced

3 garlic cloves, peeled and minced

2 jalapeño or serrano chiles, seeds and ribs removed, and finely chopped

3 tablespoons chili powder

1 tablespoon ground cumin

2 teaspoons dried oregano

1¼ pounds ground turkey

2 (14.5-ounce) cans no-salt-added crushed tomatoes in tomato puree

½ cup dry white wine

4 cups cooked black beans

Freshly ground black pepper to taste

3 cups cooked brown or white rice, hot

1. Heat oil in a saucepan over medium-high heat, swirling to coat the pan. Add onion, green bell pepper, garlic, and chiles to the pan. Cook over medium-high heat, stirring frequently, for 3 minutes, or until onion is translucent. Add chili powder, cumin, and oregano to the pan, and cook for 1 minute, stirring constantly.

2. Add turkey to the pan, breaking up lumps with a fork. Add tomatoes and wine, and stir well.

3. Bring to a boil and simmer mixture, partially covered, for 30 minutes, stirring occasionally. Add beans, and simmer for an additional 15 minutes, or until thick. Season to taste with pepper, and serve immediately over rice.

Note: The dish can be cooked up to 2 days in advance and refrigerated, tightly covered. Reheat it over low heat, covered, until hot.

Each serving contains:

156 MG SODIUM | 391 calories | 103 calories from fat | 11.5 g fat | 2 g saturated fat | 31 g protein | 39 g carbohydrates

Variations:
- Substitute ground beef for the turkey, and substitute red wine for the white wine.
- Substitute ¾-inch cubes of firm tofu for the beef; add tofu to the pan at the same time as the beans.
- Add 1–2 additional hot chiles.

Adding the spices to a skillet and cooking them briefly before adding liquid ingredients is a time-honored way to release the maximum flavor from them and take away any potential harsh quality.

Creamy Chicken and Macaroni Casserole

While cheese is relatively high in sodium, this casserole to use up left-over cooked chicken is as creamy as a mac' and cheese, and it's also loaded with lots of healthful vegetables to make this a one-dish meal.

Yield: 6 servings | **Active time:** 15 minutes | **Start to finish:** 45 minutes

$\frac{1}{2}$ pound macaroni

5 tablespoons unsalted butter, divided

1 medium onion, peeled and diced

2 garlic cloves, peeled and minced

2 celery ribs, rinsed, trimmed, and diced

$\frac{1}{2}$ pound mushrooms, wiped with a damp paper towel, trimmed, and sliced

$\frac{1}{2}$ green bell pepper, seeds and ribs removed, and diced

$\frac{1}{3}$ cup all-purpose flour

$2\frac{1}{2}$ cups whole milk

2 tablespoons chopped fresh parsley

1 teaspoon herbes de Provence

Freshly ground black pepper to taste

3 cups cooked diced chicken

1. Preheat the oven to 375°F, and grease a 9 x 13-inch baking pan. Bring a large pot of salted water to a boil, and cook macaroni according to package directions. Drain, and return macaroni to the pan.

2. Melt 2 tablespoons butter in a large skillet over medium-high heat. Add onion, garlic, celery, mushrooms, and green bell pepper. Cook, stirring frequently, for 5–7 minutes, or until vegetables soften. Remove the pan from the heat, and add vegetables to the pan with macaroni.

3. Melt remaining butter in saucepan over low heat. Stir in flour, and cook, stirring constantly, for 2 minutes. Slow whisk in milk, and bring to a boil over medium heat, whisking constantly. Stir in parsley and herbes de Provence, and simmer 1 minute. Season to taste with pepper, and pour sauce into the pan with macaroni and vegetables. Fold in chicken.

4. Scrape mixture into the prepared baking pan, and level top with a rubber spatula. Cover pan with aluminum foil, and bake for 10 minutes. Remove foil, and bake an additional 15 minutes, or until hot and bubbly. Serve immediately.

Note: The dish can be prepared for baking up to 2 days in advance and refrigerated, tightly covered. Add 10 minutes to covered baking time if the dish is chilled.

Each serving contains:

111 MG SODIUM | 444 calories | 142 calories from fat | 16 g fat | 8.5 g saturated fat | 32 g protein | 42 g carbohydrates

Variation:

- Substitute 3 (4.5-ounce) cans low-sodium light tuna, drained, for the chicken.

When pasta is to be baked for more than 1 hour, such as in a classic lasagna, it's best to undercook the noodles by a few minutes to ensure they won't get mushy. But in a casserole such as this one made with cooked chicken and baked for only 25 minutes, the pasta should be cooked to the proper state of al dente.

Spanish Chicken Salad

Many dishes in traditional Spanish cooking include succulent fresh oranges, so a salad such as this one is a good way to add some fruit servings to your day. The smoked paprika gives the chicken a grilled flavor, even though it's sautéed on the stove.

Yield: 6 servings | **Active time:** 20 minutes | **Start to finish:** 50 minutes, including 30 minutes for marinating

- 1¼ pounds boneless, skinless chicken breast halves
- ¾ cup orange juice
- 1 small onion, peeled and diced
- 3 garlic cloves, peeled and minced
- 2 tablespoons smoked Spanish paprika
- Freshly ground black pepper to taste
- ¼ cup olive oil, divided
- 6 cups bite-sized pieces iceberg lettuce or romaine, rinsed and dried
- 2 navel oranges, peeled and sliced
- 2 small fennel bulbs, stem trimmed, stalks discarded, cored, and thinly sliced

1. Rinse chicken and pat dry with paper towels. Trim all visible fat from chicken and cut it into thin slices against the grain. Combine orange juice, onion, garlic, paprika, and pepper in a jar with a tight-fitting lid. Shake well. Add 1 tablespoon oil, and shake well again. Pour ½ of dressing into a heavy resealable plastic bag. Add chicken, and marinate at room temperature for 30 minutes, turning the bag occasionally.
2. Place lettuce on a serving platter or individual plates, and arrange orange and fennel slices on top.
3. Heat remaining oil in a large skillet over medium-high heat, swirling to coat the pan. Drain chicken from marinade, and pat dry on paper towels. Discard marinade. Cook chicken, stirring constantly, for 3 minutes, or until chicken is cooked through and no longer pink. Place chicken on top of salad, drizzle salad with remaining dressing, and serve immediately.

Note: The chicken can marinate for up to 4 hours refrigerated, and the remaining dressing can be made at that time and kept at room temperature.

Each serving contains:

119 MG SODIUM | 249 calories | 70 calories from fat | 8 g fat | 1 g saturated fat | 26 g protein | 21 g carbohydrates

Variation:

- Substitute 1¼ pounds boneless pork loin for the chicken.

When you trim the ribs off of fennel bulbs before using them, they should certainly not go to waste. Use them in place of celery in salads and soups.

Chapter 8:
Meaty Matters

A portion of beef contains about 50 mg of sodium, and pork contains even less. So hearty meat dishes are certainly consistent with your low-sodium diet. Those are the recipes you'll find in this chapter.

Every cuisine seems to have ways to fix those less expensive cuts of meat that require long cooking in liquid to reach that magical status of "fork tender." A benefit of this style of cooking is that the liquid in which the meats are braised can be filled with ingredients that give the resulting food a rich flavor.

While most of the beef recipes in this chapter are for stews, there are many pork recipes that flavor "the other white meat" and then quickly roast it or grill it.

CREATIVE CUTTING

Compared to the precision needed to cut a whole chicken into its component parts, boning and cutting meat for the recipes in this chapter is a free-for-all. The bones should be removed, however. Bones slow down the cooking process for stews because they absorb heat that should be channeled to tenderizing the meats, and because they take up space, you need more liquid to braise dishes. The extra cooking time also adds to your cost. But do save any bones for making Beef Stock (recipe on page 27); unfortunately pork bones do not make a good stock.

The first step of boning is to cut away the bones. Then cut away any large areas of fat that can be easily discarded. The last step is to decide how the remaining boneless meat should be cut. The rule is to cut across the grain rather than with the grain. The reason for this is that meat becomes more tender if the ends of the fibers are exposed to the liquid and heat. If you're not sure which way the grain runs, make a test slice. You should see the ends of fibers if you cut across the grain.

PROCEDURAL PROWESS

The one major principle for almost all meat dishes is the initial browning of the meat, which means cooking the meat quickly over moderately high heat. This causes the surface of the food to brown. In the case of cubes of beef for stew, browning seals in the juices and keeps the interior moist; for ground meats, browning gives food an appetizing color, allows you to drain off some of the inherent saturated fat, and also gives dishes a rich flavor.

While larger pieces can be browned under an oven broiler, ground meats are browned in a skillet. Crumble the meat in a skillet over medium-high heat. Break up the lumps with a meat fork or the back of a spoon as it browns, and then stir it around frequently until all lumps are brown and no pink remains. At that point, it's easy to remove it from the pan with a slotted spoon and discard the grease from the pan. You can then use the pan again without washing it for any pre-cooking of other ingredients.

CUTTING BACK ON FAT

In addition to cost—because meat to be braised tends to be less expensive than cuts that are grilled or broiled—another benefit of cooking meat in sauces is that it's possible to remove a great percentage of the saturated fat. It's easy to find and discard this "bad fat," both before and after cooking.

On raw meat, the fat is easy to spot. It's the white stuff around the red stuff. Cut it off with a sharp paring knife, and you're done. However, some fat remains in the tissue of the red meat, and much of this saturated fat is released during the cooking process. There are ways to discard it when the food is either hot or cold.

If you're cooking in advance and refrigerating a dish, all the fat rises to the top and hardens once chilled. Just scrape it off, throw it away, and you're done. The same principle of fat rising to the surface is true when food is hot, but it's a bit harder to eliminate it. Tilt the pan, and the fat will form a puddle on the lower side. It's then easier to scoop it off with a soup ladle. When you're down to too little to scoop off, level the pan and blot the top with paper towels.

Beef Fajitas

Fajitas (pronounced *fah-HEE-taz*) are authentically Mexican, but have also been absorbed into Southwestern cooking. These use economical sirloin tips, which are one of the best buys in the meat case, and blend them with the traditional sautéed onions and peppers.

Yield: 6 servings | **Active time:** 25 minutes | **Start to finish:** 25 minutes

1 pound sirloin tips
¼ cup olive oil, divided
1 large red onion, peeled and thinly sliced
1 large green bell pepper, seeds and ribs removed, and thinly sliced
2 jalapeño or serrano chiles, seeds and ribs removed, and finely chopped
3 garlic cloves, peeled and minced
2 medium ripe tomatoes, rinsed, cored, seeded, and diced
¼ cup lime juice
2 teaspoons ground cumin
¼ cup chopped fresh cilantro
Freshly ground black pepper to taste
12 (6-inch) flour tortillas
Garnish (optional):
Sour cream
Summer Tomato Salsa (recipe on page 68)
Guacamole (recipe on page 69)

1. Rinse beef and pat dry with paper towels. Cut beef into ½-inch slices across the grain.
2. Heat 2 tablespoons oil in a large skillet over medium-high heat. Add beef and cook, stirring frequently, for 1½–2 minutes, or to desired doneness. Remove beef from the skillet with a slotted spoon, set aside, and keep warm. Discard fat from the skillet, and wipe out the skillet with paper towels.
3. Heat remaining oil in the skillet over medium-high heat. Add onion, green bell pepper, chiles, and garlic. Cook, stirring frequently, for 4–6 minutes, or until onion is soft. Add tomato, and cook for 1 minute. Add lime juice, cumin, cilantro, and beef, and heat through, stirring constantly. Season to taste with pepper.

4. Wrap tortillas in plastic wrap and microwave on High (100 percent power) for 20–30 seconds, or until warm and pliable. To serve, roll up filling in tortillas, and serve with small bowls of sour cream, salsa, and guacamole, if using. Serve immediately.

Note: The vegetable mixture can be made 6 hours in advance and kept at room temperature. Sauté the beef just prior to serving.

Each serving contains:

82 MG SODIUM | 438 calories | 193 calories from fat | 21.5 g fat | 4 g saturated fat | 23 g protein | 34 g carbohydrates

Variation:
- Substitute boneless, skinless chicken for the beef. Cook the chicken for 4–5 minutes, or until cooked through and no longer pink.

Cumin, pronounced *KOO-men*, is frequently found in markets under its Spanish name, *comino*. The seeds from which it's ground are the dried fruit from a plant in the parsley family, which is very aromatic. It's one of the major ingredients in commercial chili powder, so you can always substitute chili powder if necessary.

Greek Beef Stew

Many cuisines around the world, including Greek, use cinnamon as a savory spice as well as an addition to sweet baked goods. This stew has a hint of cinnamon, as well as a slight sweet and sour flavor. Serve it over orzo, or some other small pasta, along with a tossed salad.

Yield: 6 servings | **Active time:** 25 minutes | **Start to finish:** 3½ hours

1 (2-pound) chuck roast, trimmed and cut into 1-inch cubes (or 1½ pounds stewing beef)
2 tablespoons olive oil
1 medium onion, peeled and chopped
3 garlic cloves, peeled and minced
1 green bell pepper, seeds and ribs removed, and thinly sliced
2 teaspoons dried oregano
2 teaspoons ground cumin
1¼ cups dry red wine
½ cup Beef Stock (recipe on page 27)
2 tablespoons balsamic vinegar
2 tablespoons firmly packed light brown sugar
1 (6-ounce) can no-salt-added tomato paste
¼ cup chopped fresh parsley
3 carrots, peeled and cut into 1-inch chunks
3 celery ribs, rinsed, trimmed, and cut into 1-inch sections
2 bay leaves
2 (2-inch) cinnamon sticks
½ cup raisins
1 tablespoon cornstarch
2 tablespoons cold water
Freshly ground black pepper to taste

1. Preheat the oven broiler, and line a broiler pan with heavy-duty aluminum foil. Rinse beef and pat dry with paper towels. Broil beef for 3 minutes per side, or until browned. Set aside, and preheat the oven to 350°F.

2. Heat oil in a Dutch oven over medium-high heat. Add onion, garlic, and green pepper. Cook, stirring frequently, for 3 minutes, or until onion is translucent. Add oregano and cumin, and cook over low heat, stirring constantly, for 1 minute.

3. Combine wine, stock, vinegar, brown sugar, tomato paste, and parsley in a mixing bowl. Stir well to dissolve tomato paste. Pour mixture into the Dutch oven, and add beef, carrots, celery, bay leaves, cinnamon sticks, and raisins.

4. Bring to a boil on top of the stove, and then bake, covered, for 2½ hours, or until beef and vegetables are tender.

5. Spoon off as much fat as possible from surface of stew. Combine cornstarch and water in a small cup. Add mixture to the Dutch oven, and cook on top of the stove for 2–3 minutes, or until slightly thickened. Remove and discard bay leaves and cinnamon sticks. Season to taste with pepper, and serve immediately.

Note: The beef can be made up to 2 days in advance and refrigerated, tightly covered. Reheat it over low heat or in a 350°F oven for 30 minutes, or until hot.

Each serving contains:

104 MG SODIUM | 355 calories | 148 calories from fat | 16 g fat | 6 g saturated fat | 17 g protein | 29 g carbohydrates

Variation:

- Lamb shanks or lamb shoulder chops are about the most affordable version of that richly flavored meat, and they work wonderfully in this recipe. The cooking time does not change.

I like to use cinnamon sticks in slowly braised dishes because the flavor remains stronger, and the sticks do not color the liquid in the same way as ground cinnamon. But if all you have is ground cinnamon, use ½ teaspoon instead of a stick.

Caribbean Beef Stew

Coconut milk is used in tropical cuisines where coconuts grow, so it's found in the Caribbean as well as in Asian dishes. In this recipe, the creamy coconut milk blends wonderfully with the fiery chiles and spices. Serve it over rice.

Yield: 6 servings | **Active time:** 20 minutes | **Start to finish:** 3 hours

> 1 (2-pound) chuck roast, trimmed and cut into 1-inch cubes (or 1½ pounds stewing beef)
> 2 tablespoons vegetable oil
> 3 large onions, peeled and diced
> 4 garlic cloves, peeled and minced
> 2 large jalapeño or serrano chiles, seeds and ribs removed, and finely chopped
> 3 tablespoons grated fresh ginger
> 2 tablespoons ground coriander
> 1 tablespoon ground cumin
> 1 (14-ounce) can light coconut milk
> 2 cups Beef Stock (recipe on page 27)
> 2 carrots, peeled and cut into 1-inch sections
> 2 parsnips, peeled and cut into 1-inch sections
> 1 celery root, peeled and cut into 1-inch dice
> 1 tablespoon cornstarch
> 2 tablespoons cold water
> Freshly ground black pepper to taste

1. Preheat the oven broiler, and line a broiler pan with heavy-duty aluminum foil. Rinse beef and pat dry with paper towels. Broil beef for 3 minutes per side, or until browned, and set aside. Preheat the oven to 350°F.

2. Heat oil in a Dutch oven over medium-high heat. Add onions, garlic, chiles, and ginger. Cook, stirring frequently, for 3 minutes, or until onion is translucent. Add coriander and cumin and cook over low heat for 1 minute, stirring constantly. Add coconut milk and stock, and stir well. Add beef, carrots, parsnips, and celery root.

3. Bring to a boil on top of the stove, and then bake, covered, for 2½ hours, or until beef and vegetables are tender.

4. Spoon off as much fat as possible from surface of stew. Combine cornstarch and water in a small cup. Add mixture to the Dutch oven, and cook on top of the stove for 2–3 minutes, or until slightly thickened. Season to taste with pepper, and serve immediately.

Note: The beef can be made up to 2 days in advance and refrigerated, tightly covered. Reheat it over low heat or in a 350°F oven for 30 minutes, or until hot.

Each serving contains:

146 MG SODIUM | 512 calories | 267 calories from fat | 30 g fat | 13 g saturated fat | 29 g protein | 21 g carbohydrates

Variation:
- Substitute pork loin for the beef, and substitute chicken stock for the beef stock. Reduce the cooking time to 2 hours.

You'll notice that I always specify light coconut milk in recipes, because the difference in the calorie count is really astounding. Full-fat coconut milk has about three times the calories of light coconut milk, depending on the brand.

Belgian Beef Stew (*Carbonnades à la Flamande*)

Belgium is a country known for its beer and not for its wine, so it makes sense that they would use it in cooking too. This is a classic stew, with lots of sweet caramelized onions as a contrast to the bitter beer. Serve it with some buttered egg noodles.

Yield: 6 servings | **Active time:** 20 minutes | **Start to finish:** 3 hours

> 1 (2-pound) chuck roast, trimmed and cut into 1-inch cubes (or 1½ pounds stewing beef)
> 3 tablespoons vegetable oil
> 4 large onions, peeled and thinly sliced
> 2 garlic cloves, peeled and minced
> 2 teaspoons granulated sugar
> Freshly ground black pepper to taste
> 1½ cups Beef Stock (recipe on page 27)
> 1 (12-ounce) can or bottle lager beer
> 2 tablespoons firmly packed dark brown sugar
> 2 tablespoons chopped fresh parsley
> 1 teaspoon dried thyme
> 1 bay leaf
> 1 tablespoon cornstarch
> 1 tablespoon cold water

1. Preheat the oven broiler, and line a broiler pan with heavy-duty aluminum foil. Rinse beef and pat dry with paper towels. Arrange beef in a single layer on the foil, and broil for 3 minutes per side, or until beef is lightly browned.

2. Heat oil in a Dutch oven over medium heat. Add onions and garlic, toss to coat with fat, and cook, covered, for 10 minutes. Uncover the pan, raise the heat to medium-high, and sprinkle onions with sugar and pepper. Cook, stirring occasionally, for 10–12 minutes, or until onions are lightly browned.

3. Return beef to the pan, and stir in stock, beer, brown sugar, parsley, thyme, and bay leaf. Bring to a boil on top of the stove, stirring occasionally.

4. Cover the pan, and bake for 2–2½ hours, or until meat is tender. Spoon off as much fat as possible from surface. Combine cornstarch and water in a small cup, and stir into stew. Cook over low heat for 2 minutes, or until slightly thickened. Serve immediately.

Note: The dish can be made up to 2 days in advance and refrigerated, tightly covered. Reheat it over low heat or in a 350°F oven for 30 minutes, or until hot.

Each serving contains:

127 MG SODIUM | 332 calories | 122 calories from fat | 14 g fat | 4.5 g saturated fat | 30 g protein | 18 g carbohydrates

Variation:
- Substitute Guinness Stout or dark ale for the beer.

Cooking onions over low heat and covered for a brief time is called "sweating" in cooking lingo. This initial cooking draws out much of the onions' bitterness and softens them so that they brown more easily.

Beef Stew Stroganoff

Beef Stroganoff was named for a nineteenth-century Russian diplomat, Count Paul Stroganoff; it became a hallmark of what Americans called "continental cuisine" in the mid-twentieth century. While the original Beef Stroganoff is a quickly sautéed dish, this long-simmered braise has the same flavors of sour cream and a rich tomato sauce. Serve it over buttered egg noodles with a steamed green vegetable.

Yield: 6 servings | **Active time:** 15 minutes | **Start to finish:** 3 hours

> 1 (2-pound) chuck roast, trimmed and cut into 1-inch cubes (or 1½ pounds stewing beef)
> Freshly ground black pepper to taste
> ½ cup all-purpose flour
> 2 tablespoons vegetable oil
> 2 tablespoons unsalted butter
> 2 large onions, peeled and diced
> 3 garlic cloves, peeled and minced
> ½ pound mushrooms, wiped with a damp paper towel, trimmed, and sliced
> 2 tablespoons paprika
> 2 cups Beef Stock (recipe on page 27)
> 3 tablespoons no-salt-added tomato paste
> 2 tablespoons chopped fresh parsley
> 1 tablespoon Marvelous Mustard (recipe on page 40)
> ½ cup sour cream

1. Preheat the oven to 350°F. Rinse beef and pat dry with paper towels. Season meat to taste with pepper, and dust meat with flour, shaking off any excess into the sink or a garbage can. Heat oil in a Dutch oven over medium-high heat. Add beef, and cook, turning pieces with tongs, until brown on all sides. Remove meat from the pan with slotted spoon, and set aside.

2. Add butter to the pan. When butter melts, add onions and garlic, and cook, stirring frequently, for 3 minutes, or until onion is translucent. Add mushrooms, and cook for 2 minutes more. Add paprika to the pan, and cook for 1 minute, stirring constantly.

3. Add stock, tomato paste, parsley, and mustard to the pan. Stir well, return meat to the pan, and bring to a boil on top of the stove, stirring occasionally.

4. Cover the pan, and bake for 2–2½ hours, or until meat is tender. Spoon off as much fat as possible from surface. Stir in sour cream, and season to taste with pepper. Do not allow dish to boil. Serve immediately.

Note: The dish can be made up to 2 days in advance and refrigerated, tightly covered. Reheat it over low heat or in a 350°F oven for 30 minutes, or until hot.

Each serving contains:

152 MG SODIUM | 350 calories | 177 calories from fat | 20 g fat | 8 g saturated fat | 32 g protein | 9 g carbohydrates

Variation:
- Substitute boneless, skinless chicken thighs, and reduce the cooking time to 1½–2 hours, or until chicken is cooked through and no longer pink.

Beef Braised in Red Wine with Potatoes and Vegetables (Boeuf Bourguignon)

While cooking with wine is more expensive than cooking with stock, a "cooking wine" hardly needs to be of high quality; forget the old adage that "you never cook with a wine you wouldn't drink." This hearty stew is perfect for a fall or winter night.

Yield: 6 servings | **Active time:** 20 minutes | **Start to finish:** 3 hours

1 (2-pound) chuck roast, trimmed and cut into 1-inch cubes (or 1½ pounds stewing beef)
Freshly ground black pepper to taste
½ cup all-purpose flour
¼ cup olive oil
1 large onion, peeled and diced
3 garlic cloves, peeled and minced
½ pound small mushrooms, wiped with a damp paper towel, trimmed, and halved if large
2 cups dry red wine
1 cup Beef Stock (recipe on page 27)
2 tablespoons no-salt-added tomato paste
2 tablespoons chopped fresh parsley
1 tablespoon herbes de Provence
1 bay leaf
2 carrots, peeled and cut into 1-inch chunks
1 pound baby red potatoes, scrubbed, or small red potatoes cut into quarters

1. Preheat the oven to 350°F. Rinse beef and pat dry with paper towels. Season meat to taste with pepper, and dust meat with flour, shaking off any excess into the sink or a garbage can. Heat oil in Dutch oven over medium-high heat. Add beef, and cook, turning pieces with tongs, until brown on all sides. Remove from pan with slotted spoon, and set aside.

2. Add onion and garlic to pan, and cook, stirring frequently, for 3 minutes, or until onion is translucent. Add mushrooms, and cook for 2 minutes more. Add wine, stock, tomato paste, parsley, herbes de Provence, and bay leaf to the pan. Stir well, return meat to the pan, and bring to a boil on top of the stove, stirring occasionally.

3. Cover the pan, and bake for 1 hour. Remove the pan from the oven, add carrots and potatoes, and bake for an additional 1½ hours, or until meat and potatoes are tender. Spoon off as much fat as possible from surface, remove and discard bay leaf, season to taste with pepper, and serve immediately.

Note: The dish can be made up to 2 days in advance and refrigerated, tightly covered. Reheat it over low heat or in a 350°F oven for 30 minutes, or until hot.

Each serving contains:

150 MG SODIUM | 396 calories | 122 calories from fat | 14 g fat | 4 g saturated fat | 33 g protein | 23 g carbohydrates

> When you coat food with flour prior to browning it in oil, the oil cooks the proteins in the flour so they'll lightly thicken the pan juices with no "floury" taste. The flour also creates browner beef. However, some sort of fat like butter or oil is necessary when browning flour, which is why stews and roasts browned under the broiler are thickened most often with cornstarch.

Spicy Chili

Here's a wonderful rendition of this American favorite; it's made with spicy chiles as well as other herbs and spices. Serve it over rice, with the typical garnishes of onions and sour cream.

Yield: 6 servings | **Active time:** 15 minutes | **Start to finish:** 40 minutes

3 tablespoons olive oil, divided
1 pound lean ground beef
1 large onion, peeled and diced
3 garlic cloves, peeled and minced
1 large green bell pepper, seeds and ribs removed, and chopped
2 jalapeño or serrano chiles, seeds and ribs removed, and finely chopped
2 tablespoons all-purpose flour
3 tablespoons chili powder
2 tablespoons ground cumin
2 teaspoons dried oregano
2 teaspoons unsweetened cocoa powder (not Dutch processed)
2 (14.5-ounce) cans no-salt-added diced tomatoes, undrained
3 cups cooked kidney beans or pinto beans
Cayenne to taste
3 cups cooked brown or white rice, hot

1. Heat 1 tablespoon oil in a large saucepan over medium-high heat. Add beef, breaking up lumps with a fork. Cook beef, stirring frequently, for 3 minutes, or until browned. Remove beef from the pan with a slotted spoon, and set aside. Discard fat from the saucepan.
2. Heat remaining oil in the saucepan. Add onion, garlic, bell pepper, and chiles. Cook, stirring frequently, for 3 minutes, or until onion is translucent. Stir in flour, chili powder, cumin, oregano, and cocoa. Cook over low heat, stirring frequently, for 1 minute.
3. Return beef to the pan, add tomatoes, and bring to a boil over medium heat. Simmer chili, uncovered, stirring occasionally, for 20 minutes, or until thick. Add beans, and cook for an additional 5 minutes. Season to taste with cayenne, and serve immediately over rice.

Note: The dish can be prepared up to 2 days in advance and refrigerated, tightly covered. Reheat it, covered, in a saucepan over low heat until hot, stirring occasionally.

Each serving contains:

137 MG SODIUM | 337 calories | 111 calories from fat | 12 g fat | 4 g satu-
rated fat | 25 g protein | 34 g carbohydrates

Variations:
- Substitute ground turkey or ground pork for the beef.
- There's a related dish in Mexican cooking called *picadillo*. Omit the oregano, and add ½ teaspoon ground cinnamon, ½ cup rai-sins, and 1 tablespoon cider vinegar to the chili.

Many authentic Mexican dishes contain a small amount of unsweetened cocoa powder. It adds richness and intensity to the sauce, but it's not noticeable in the finished dish.

Grilled Pork with Tropical Salsa

While salsa is synonymous with tomato or tomatillo in Mexican cooking, creative chefs have begun using a variety of succulent tropical fruits in them as well. The sweet and sour salsa made with orange and mango is terrific with the marinated pork. Serve it with some corn tortillas.

Yield: 6 servings | **Active time:** 15 minutes | **Start to finish:** 50 minutes

PORK

1½ pounds boneless pork loin
¾ cup orange juice
2 tablespoons lime juice
1 tablespoon smoked Spanish paprika
2 teaspoons ground cumin
Freshly ground black pepper to taste
2 tablespoons olive oil

SALSA

1 navel orange
1 ripe mango, peeled and chopped
½ small red onion, peeled and chopped
3 tablespoons chopped fresh cilantro
2 jalapeño or serrano chiles, seeds and ribs removed, and finely chopped
3 tablespoons lime juice
Cayenne to taste

1. Rinse pork and pat dry with paper towels. Cut pork into 6 slices. Combine orange juice, lime juice, paprika, cumin, and pepper in a heavy resealable plastic bag. Mix well, add oil, and mix well again. Add pork, and marinate for 30 minutes at room temperature, turning the bag occasionally.
2. Light a charcoal or gas grill, or preheat the oven broiler.
3. While pork marinates, make salsa. Grate 1 tablespoon zest from orange, then cut peel and white pith from orange and cut it into ½-inch cubes. Combine orange, mango, onion, cilantro, chiles, and lime juice in a mixing bowl, and stir well. Season to taste with cayenne, and set aside.

4. Remove pork from marinade, and discard marinade. Grill or broil pork for 3 minutes per side, or to desired doneness. Serve immediately, garnishing each pork slice with salsa.

Note: The salsa can be prepared up to 1 day in advance and refrigerated, tightly covered. Allow it to reach room temperature before serving.

Each serving contains:

57.5 MG SODIUM | 245 calories | 95 calories from fat | 10.5 g fat | 4 g saturated fat | 26 g protein | 12 g carbohydrates

Variations:
- Substitute papaya or pineapple for the mango.
- Substitute boneless, skinless chicken breast halves for the pork. Cook chicken to an internal temperature of 165°F on an instant-read thermometer, or until it is cooked through and no longer pink.

> Mangoes are difficult to cut because of the elliptical pit in the center. The best way to get off all the flesh is to cut along each side of the pit so you get 2 large chunks of fruit, and then take the small bits of flesh still clinging to the pit.

Italian Pork Loin with Garlic and Rosemary

While traveling in Umbria a few summers ago I fell in love with a regional dish called *porchetta,* which is pork roasted with lots of garlic and rosemary, and decided I had to replicate it in my kitchen. Serve this tasty pork with some pasta tossed with olive oil and garlic, and a tossed salad.

Yield: 6 servings | **Active time:** 15 minutes | **Start to finish:** 1 hour

1 (1½-pound) boneless pork loin roast
1 lemon
4 garlic cloves, peeled and minced
3 tablespoons chopped fresh rosemary
2 tablespoons olive oil
Freshly ground black pepper to taste
½ cup dry white wine

1. Preheat the oven to 450°F. Rinse pork and pat dry with paper towels. Cut slits into pork at 2-inch intervals that go halfway through roast. Grate zest from lemon, and squeeze juice from fruit.
2. Combine lemon zest, garlic, rosemary, oil, and pepper in a small mixing bowl. Stir well, and stuff mixture into slits created in pork roast. Sprinkle outside of roast with additional pepper. Place pork in a metal roasting pan.
3. Bake pork for 10 minutes, then reduce the heat to 350°F, and continue to roast pork for an additional 25–40 minutes, or until an instant-read thermometer registers 145°F.
4. Remove roast from the oven, place it on a platter, and allow it to rest for 10 minutes, lightly covered with aluminum foil. Place the roasting pan on the stove, and add wine and lemon juice. Cook over medium-high heat for 3 minutes, stirring to incorporate any brown bits into sauce. To serve, slice pork thinly, adding any juices to sauce. Spoon sauce over pork, and serve immediately.

Note: The pork can be prepared for roasting up to 1 day in advance and refrigerated, tightly covered. Allow pork to sit at room temperature while oven heats. The pork can also be served cold.

Each serving contains:

58 MG SODIUM | 172 calories | 49 calories from fat | 5 g fat | 1 g saturated fat | 26 g protein | 2 g carbohydrates

Variation:

- Substitute boned and rolled turkey breast for the pork. Roast turkey to an internal temperature of 165°F.

It's important to let all roasted meat rest; its internal temperature will rise about 10 degrees while resting and the juices will be reabsorbed into the fibers. The same rule applies to roast whole chickens or turkeys, but not to chicken cut into serving pieces.

Spanish Pork with Garbanzo Beans

Topping off this flavorful pork with a sprinkling of garlic-laced parsley adds a fresh accent to the long-simmered dish, and the smoked paprika adds its heady nuance to the sauce. Serve this on top of rice, with a tossed salad to complete the meal.

Yield: 6 servings | **Active time:** 25 minutes | **Start to finish:** 2 hours

1¼ pounds boneless pork loin, cut into 1-inch cubes
2 tablespoons olive oil
1 large onion, peeled and diced
6 garlic cloves, peeled and minced, divided
1 large carrot, peeled and sliced
1 celery rib, rinsed, trimmed, and sliced
3 tablespoons smoked Spanish paprika
1 tablespoon chili powder
2 teaspoons ground cumin
1 (14.5-ounce) can no-salt-added diced tomatoes, undrained
1¼ cups Chicken Stock (recipe on page 26)
½ cup dry sherry
2 tablespoons no-salt-added tomato paste
1 bay leaf
3 cups cooked garbanzo beans
¼ cup chopped fresh parsley
Freshly ground black pepper to taste
3 cups cooked brown or white rice, hot

1. Preheat the oven broiler, and line a broiler pan with heavy-duty aluminum foil. Brown pork for 3–5 minutes per side, or until lightly browned. Set aside, and preheat the oven to 375°F.
2. Heat oil in a Dutch oven over medium-high heat. Add onion, ½ of garlic, carrot, and celery. Cook, stirring frequently, for 3 minutes, or until onion is translucent. Add paprika, chili powder, and cumin, and cook for 1 minute, stirring constantly.
3. Combine tomatoes, stock, sherry, and tomato paste in a mixing bowl. Stir well to dissolve tomato paste. Add tomato mixture, pork, and bay leaf to Dutch oven.
4. Bring to a boil on top of the stove, and then bake, covered, for 45 minutes. Add beans, and bake for an additional 45 minutes, or until pork and vegetables are tender.

5. While pork cooks, combine remaining garlic and parsley in a small bowl, and set aside. Remove and discard bay leaf, season to taste with pepper, and serve immediately over rice, sprinkling each serving with parsley mixture.

Note: The pork can be prepared up to 2 days in advance and refrigerated, tightly covered. Reheat it, covered, in a 350°F oven for 30 minutes, or until hot.

Each serving contains:

132 MG SODIUM | 478 calories | 78 calories from fat | 9 g fat | 1 g saturated fat | 37 g protein | 65 g carbohydrates

Variation:
- Substitute 1 (3½–4-pound) frying chicken, cut into serving pieces, for the pork. The cooking time will remain the same; cook the chicken until it is cooked through and no longer pink.

Braised Pork Chops with Red Cabbage

Cabbage is one of the oldest vegetables in recorded history, although its stature has ranged from lowly to esteemed depending on the culture. In this case, pork chops become meltingly tender when cooked with bright red cabbage, and the dish has a slightly sweet and sour flavor. Some oven-roasted potatoes go well with it.

Yield: 6 servings | **Active time:** 15 minutes | **Start to finish:** 1 hour

1½ pounds boneless pork loin
Freshly ground black pepper to taste
2 tablespoons vegetable oil
1 medium onion, peeled and chopped
2 Golden Delicious apples, cored, peeled, and cut into ½-inch dice
1 cup Chicken Stock (recipe on page 26)
½ cup dry red wine
2 tablespoons cider vinegar
3 tablespoons firmly packed dark brown sugar
1 (3-inch) cinnamon stick
1 bay leaf
1 (2-pound) head red cabbage, cored and shredded
⅓ cup red currant jelly

1. Rinse pork and pat dry with paper towels. Trim pork of visible fat, and cut into 6 slices. Sprinkle slices with pepper. Heat oil in a deep-sided skillet over medium-high heat. Add pork and cook, turning pieces with tongs, until brown on both sides. Remove pork from the pan with tongs and set aside.

2. Add onion and apples and cook, stirring frequently, for 3 minutes, or until onion is translucent. Add stock, wine, vinegar, sugar, cinnamon stick, and bay leaf. Bring to a boil and stir in the cabbage. Bring to a boil and cook, uncovered, for 5 minutes.

3. Bury chops in cabbage, cover the pan, and cook over low heat for 30–45 minutes, or until the cabbage and pork are tender. Remove pork from the pan, remove and discard cinnamon stick and bay leaf, and stir jelly into the cabbage. Cook, uncovered, over medium heat for 10 minutes, or until the liquid reduces and becomes syrupy. Return chops to pan and heat through.

Note: The dish can be cooked up to 2 days in advance and refrigerated, tightly covered. Reheat it over low heat until simmering.

Each serving contains:

115 MG SODIUM | 324 calories | 54 calories from fat | 6 g fat | 2 g saturated fat | 29 g protein | 38 g carbohydrates

Variation:
- Substitute boneless, skinless chicken thighs for the pork; the cooking time will remain the same.

Cabbage, along with cauliflower, broccoli, and Brussels sprouts, ia a great vegetable to eat for its medicinal properties. The family is very high in vitamin C, as well as glutamine, an amino acid that has anti-inflammatory properties.

Old-Fashioned Pork and Beans

A half-cup serving of canned baked beans can list upwards of 500 mg of sodium, but there's no reason to give them up; this recipe comes to the rescue. I sometimes double the recipe except for the amount of pork, and I freeze the leftover beans to use for future meals as a side dish.

Yield: 6 servings | **Active time:** 15 minutes | **Start to finish:** 4 hours

 1 pound dried small navy beans, rinsed
 1 pound boneless country ribs, cut into 1-inch cubes
 2 tablespoons vegetable oil
 Freshly ground black pepper to taste
 1 large onion, peeled and diced
 6 cups water
 1 cup no-salt-added ketchup
 $\frac{1}{3}$ cup molasses
 $\frac{1}{4}$ cup cider vinegar
 $\frac{1}{4}$ cup firmly packed dark brown sugar
 1 tablespoon mustard powder

1. Rinse beans in a colander and place them in a mixing bowl covered with cold water. Allow beans to soak overnight. Or place beans into a saucepan and bring to a boil over high heat. Boil 1 minute. Turn off the heat, cover the pan, and soak beans for 1 hour. With either soaking method, drain beans, discard soaking water, and begin cooking as soon as possible.

2. Preheat the oven to 350°F. Rinse pork and pat dry with paper towels. Heat oil in a Dutch oven over medium-high heat. Sprinkle pork with pepper. Add pork and cook, turning pieces with tongs, until brown on all sides. Remove pork from the pan with slotted spoon and set aside.

3. Add onion to the pan and cook, stirring frequently, for 3 minutes, or until onion is translucent. Return pork to the pan and add beans, water, ketchup, molasses, vinegar, brown sugar, and mustard powder. Bring to a boil, cover the pan, and bake for 1 hour.

4. Uncover the pan, stir, and return the pan to the oven for $2\frac{1}{2}$–3 hours, or until beans are very tender and dish is thick. Stir beans every 20 minutes. Serve immediately.

Note: The dish can be cooked up to 2 days in advance and refrigerated, tightly covered. Reheat, covered with foil, in a 350°F oven for 30 minutes, or until hot.

Each serving contains:

72 MG SODIUM | 528 calories | 69 calories from fat | 8 g fat | 2 g saturated fat | 33 g protein | 80.5 g carbohydrates

Variation:
- Substitute pure maple syrup for the molasses.

> Baked beans are so interwoven into Boston's history that it's still known as "Beantown." The original Pilgrims began the custom of starting beans on a Saturday night to eat on Sunday, because they didn't believe in cooking on the Sabbath.

Balsamic Sweet and Sour Pork

Balsamic vinegar is so inherently sweet that I drizzle it on fresh strawberries from time to time. For this quick and easy dish the balsamic is contrasted with succulent raisins with some herbs added for more interest. Serve it with pasta and a steamed green vegetable.

Yield: 6 servings | **Active time:** 15 minutes | **Start to finish:** 20 minutes

> 1½ pounds boneless pork loin
> ⅔ cup dry white wine
> ½ cup orange juice
> ½ cup balsamic vinegar
> 1 cup raisins, preferably golden raisins
> 3 tablespoons olive oil
> 2 tablespoons chopped fresh parsley
> ½ teaspoon dried thyme
> Freshly ground black pepper to taste

1. Rinse pork and pat dry with paper towels. Trim pork of all visible fat and cut into ½-inch-thick slices. Set aside.
2. Combine wine, orange juice, and vinegar in a small saucepan. Bring to a boil over high heat, then reduce the heat to low and simmer mixture, uncovered, for 5 minutes. Add raisins, remove the pan from the heat, and allow fruit to plump for 10 minutes.
3. Heat oil in a large skillet over medium-high heat. Add pork slices and cook for 1½–2 minutes per side, or until browned. Add sauce mixture, parsley, and thyme to the skillet, and boil for 1 minute. Season to taste with pepper, and serve immediately.

Note: The dish can be prepared up to 1 day in advance and refrigerated, tightly covered. To serve, reheat it, covered, over low heat, stirring occasionally.

Each serving contains:

53 MG SODIUM | 308 calories | 115 calories from fat | 13 g fat | 4 g saturated fat | 22 g protein | 23 g carbohydrates

Variation:
- Substitute thinly sliced boneless, skinless chicken breast for the pork.

Old cookbooks always used to specify to plump dried fruit in hot liquid before adding them to a dish. For recipes that require a long cooking time, like a soup or stew, that step is unnecessary because the fruit will plump as the dish cooks. But it is a good step in quick-cooking dishes such as this one.

Key West Pork Salad with Oranges

The cooking in the Florida Keys is a combination of American and Cuban with some Caribbean accents thrown in for good measure. This refreshing salad is typical of the use of colorful and flavorful fruits and vegetables found in the Keys.

Yield: 6 servings | **Active time:** 20 minutes | **Start to finish:** 40 minutes

1¼ pounds boneless pork loin

2 teaspoons ground ginger

2 teaspoons mustard powder

2 teaspoons ground coriander

Cayenne to taste

4 navel oranges

¼ cup cider vinegar

2 tablespoons chopped fresh cilantro

2 garlic cloves, peeled and minced

Freshly ground black pepper to taste

⅓ cup olive oil

6 cups bite-sized pieces romaine or iceberg lettuce, rinsed and dried

½ small red onion, peeled and thinly sliced

1 small carrot, peeled and shredded

1 celery rib, rinsed, trimmed, and sliced

1. Preheat the oven to 450°F, and line a baking pan with aluminum foil. Rinse pork and pat dry with paper towels. Trim pork of all visible fat, and cut in half lengthwise into 2 long pieces. Combine ginger, mustard, coriander, and cayenne in a small bowl. Rub mixture onto all sides of pork.

2. Roast pork for 20 minutes, or until an instant-read thermometer registers 145°F. Remove pork from the oven, and allow it to rest for 15 minutes. Then slice pork into thin slices.

3. While pork roasts, prepare salad. Cut all rind and white pith off oranges, and slice thinly. Combine vinegar, cilantro, garlic, and pepper in a jar with a tight-fitting lid. Shake well, add oil, and shake well again.

4. To serve, toss lettuce with onion, carrot, and celery in a mixing bowl, and arrange salad on individual plates or on a large platter. Arrange pork and oranges on top, and drizzle with dressing. Serve immediately.

Note: The dressing and the pork can be prepared up to 2 hours in advance and kept at room temperature. The salad ingredients can also be prepared at that time, and should be refrigerated.

Each serving contains:

65 MG SODIUM | 310 calories | 158 calories from fat | 17.5 g fat | 6 g saturated fat | 23 g protein | 16 g carbohydrates

Variation:

- Boneless, skinless chicken breasts or chicken thighs can be substituted for the pork. Roast them at 400°F for 25–30 minutes, or until an instant-read thermometer registers 165°F.

Chapter 9:
Just Desserts

Luscious cakes and cookies can be part of a low-sodium diet. Then there are pies, cream puffs, and custards too.

Both baking powder and baking soda—the most commonly used leavening agents in cakes and cookies—are loaded with sodium. In fact, a single teaspoon of baking soda contains 1,259 mg of sodium. Keep that box in the refrigerator to absorb odors, but keep it away from mixing bowls if you're trying to follow a low-sodium diet. But these desserts can be made without them.

The purpose of a leavening agent is to create bubbles of carbon dioxide that cause batters and doughs to rise and create the texture we associate with baked goods. But yeast, a natural rather than chemical leavening agent, has been accomplishing the same task for centuries, as have egg whites beaten into a stiff meringue. You'll find recipes for light-as-a-feather angel food cakes, and yeast-risen *baba au rhum,* as well as crisp cookies and fruit-filled desserts.

BAKING BASICS

While cooking is a form of art, when it comes to baking, science class enters the equation as well. While savory recipes are tolerant of virtually endless substitutions, baked goods are not. Each ingredient performs a specific function in a recipe based on a certain quantity to create a batter or dough.

These are general pointers on procedures to be used for all genres of baked goods:

- **Measure accurately.** Measure dry ingredients in dry measuring cups, which are plastic or metal, and come in sizes of $1/4$, $1/3$, $1/2$, and 1 cup. Spoon dry ingredients from the container or canister into the measuring cup, and then sweep the top with a straight edge such as the back of a knife or a spatula to measure it properly. Do not dip the cup into the canister or tap it on the counter to produce a level surface. These methods pack down the dry ingredients, and can increase the actual volume by up to 10 percent.

Tablespoons and teaspoons should also be leveled; a rounded ½ teaspoon can really measure almost 1 teaspoon. If the box or can does not have a straight edge built in, then level the excess in the spoon back into the container with the back of a knife. Measure liquids in liquid measures, which come in different sizes, but are transparent glass or plastic and have lines on the sides. To accurately measure liquids, place the measuring cup on a flat counter, and bend down to read the marked level.

- **Create consistent temperature.** All ingredients should be at room temperature unless otherwise indicated. Having all ingredients at the same temperature makes it easier to combine them into a smooth, homogeneous mixture. Adding cold liquid to a dough or batter can cause the batter to lose its unified structure by making the fat rigid.

- **Preheat the oven.** Some ovens can take up to 25 minutes to reach a high temperature, such as 450°F. The minimum heating time should be 15 minutes.

- **Plan ahead.** Read the recipe thoroughly, and assemble all your ingredients. This means that you have accounted for all ingredients required for a recipe in advance, so you don't get to a step and realize you must improvise. Assembling in advance also lessens the risk of over-mixing dough or batters, as the mixer drones on while you search for a specific spice or bag of chips.

Baba au Rhum

This is clearly an adult cake; the rum is not cooked so it has its full alcohol content—although it's not enough to feel the effects unless you eat the whole thing in one sitting. I usually serve it topped with some cooked blueberries or peaches.

Yield: 12 servings | **Active time:** 15 minutes | **Start to finish:** 2¼ hours

CAKE

½ cup whole milk
4 teaspoons (2 envelopes) active dry yeast
2 cups bread flour, divided
1 tablespoon granulated sugar
3 large eggs, at room temperature
¼ pound (1 stick) unsalted butter, melted and cooled

SYRUP

1 cup granulated sugar
1½ cups water
⅔ cup rum
½ teaspoon pure vanilla extract

1. Heat milk in a small saucepan or a microwave-safe cup to 110°F. Stir in yeast, and wait 2 minutes to allow yeast to soften. In the bowl of a standard electric mixer, combine milk-yeast mixture, ½ cup flour, and sugar. Stir to form a sponge and let rise, covered, until doubled, about 20 minutes.

2. Beating with the paddle attachment, add eggs 1 at a time, followed by remaining 1½ cups flour. When a soft dough forms, slowly beat in butter to make a smooth dough. Let dough rest for 15 minutes.

3. Grease and flour a large baba mold or 9-inch bundt cake pan. Place dough in the prepared pan, cover with plastic wrap, and let rise in a warm, draft-free place until it has nearly reached the top of the mold, about 40 minutes.

4. While baba rises, preheat the oven to 375°F. Bake baba on the middle rack of the oven for 30 minutes, or until the top is golden brown and the sides have begun to pull away from the pan slightly.

5. While baba bakes, make syrup. Place sugar and water in a small saucepan and cook over high heat until the sugar dissolves. Add rum and vanilla, and set aside.

6. Remove baba from the oven, and cool on a wire rack for 10 minutes. Set the wire rack over a platter. Using a meat fork or long skewer, poke holes all over the top of the cake. Pour warm syrup over warm cake and let sit for 5 minutes, or until the liquid is absorbed. Turn baba out onto the wire rack, and let drain over the platter for 30 minutes; pour any accumulated syrup back onto cake.

Note: The cake can be made up to 3 days in advance and refrigerated, tightly covered. Allow it to reach room temperature before serving.

Each serving contains:

25 MG SODIUM | 276 calories | 87 calories from fat | 10 g fat | 5.5 g saturated fat | 5 g protein | 35.5 g carbohydrates

Variations:
- Substitute triple sec or bourbon for the rum.
- Substitute 1 (6-ounce) can orange juice concentrate or lemon juice concentrate for the rum, and decrease the sugar to $1/2$ cup.
- Substitute light coconut milk for the whole milk, and add $3/4$ cup toasted shredded coconut to the dough.

Strawberry-Rhubarb Meringue Torte

Tart rhubarb is frequently called the "pie vegetable" because it is paired so often with fresh strawberries, which are a similar color and come to market at a similar time. In this case, the two are joined in an impressive torte that is created with layers of crunchy meringue and whipped cream.

Yield: 8 servings | **Active time:** 25 minutes | **Start to finish:** 3 hours

    4 large egg whites, at room temperature
    $1/4$ teaspoon cream of tartar
    $1\frac{1}{2}$ cups granulated sugar, divided
    1 pound fresh rhubarb, rinsed, trimmed, and chopped
    1 tablespoon cornstarch
    1 tablespoon cold water
    1 cup heavy cream
    $1/4$ cup confectioners' sugar
    $1/2$ teaspoon pure vanilla extract
    $2\frac{1}{2}$ cups sliced strawberries

1. Preheat the oven to 250°F. Line 2 baking sheets with parchment paper and, using a plate or cake pan as a guide, draw 3 (9-inch) circles on the sheets of parchment paper; 2 on one sheet and 1 on the other.

2. Place egg whites in a grease-free mixing bowl and beat at medium speed with an electric mixer until frothy. Add cream of tartar, raise the speed to high, and beat until soft peaks form. Add 1 cup sugar, 1 tablespoon at a time, and continue to beat until stiff peaks form and meringue is glossy.

3. Place equal portions of meringue in the center of each circle, and spread meringue evenly to fill circles. Bake layers for 1 hour, switching the position of the baking sheets in the oven after 30 minutes. Layers should be crisp and firm.

4. Turn off the oven and cool layers completely on the baking sheets. Remove layers from the oven and peel off the parchment paper.

5. While layers bake, prepare filling. Combine rhubarb and remaining $1/2$ cup sugar in a small saucepan, and bring to a boil over medium heat, stirring occasionally. Cook, stirring occasionally, for 10–12 minutes, or until rhubarb is tender. Combine cornstarch and water in a small cup, and add to rhubarb. Cook for 1–2 minutes, or until slightly thickened.

Puree in a food processor fitted with the steel blade or in a blender. Allow mixture to cool to room temperature.

6. Just prior to serving, place cream in a well-chilled bowl. Beat at medium speed with an electric mixer until soft peaks form. Add confectioners' sugar and vanilla, and beat until stiff peaks form.

7. To assemble, place 1 meringue layer on a serving platter and top with 1/2 of rhubarb puree. Spread with 1/3 of whipped cream, and top with 1/3 of strawberries. Repeat with remaining layers, ending with final 1/3 of whipped cream and strawberries. Serve immediately.

Note: Meringue layers may be made 1 day in advance and kept in a cool, dry place, tightly covered with plastic wrap. The rhubarb puree can be made up to 3 days ahead and refrigerated, tightly covered.

Each serving contains:

42 MG SODIUM | 303 calories | 102 calories from fat | 11 g fat | 7 g saturated fat | 3 g protein | 49.5 g carbohydrates

Variation:

- Substitute raspberries or sliced apricots or peaches for the strawberries.

Meringue is nothing more than egg whites beaten with sugar, and the purpose of the long but gentle bake time is to evaporate the water and create a crisp texture. If the weather is very humid, it can take up to 1½ hours to achieve this goal, because there's moisture in the air that must evaporate as well.

Upside-Down Caramel Apple Tart

This upside down pie, called *a tarte tatin* in classic French cooking, is the ultimate showy apple dessert, but it's really quite easy to make. It's also speedier than a pie because the apples are cooked on top of the stove before a final baking.

Yield: 8 servings | **Active time:** 20 minutes | **Start to finish:** 50 minutes

6 Golden Delicious apples, peeled, cored, and quartered, with each
quarter halved lengthwise
1½ cups granulated sugar, divided
3 tablespoons lemon juice
½ teaspoon apple pie spice
6 tablespoons (¾ stick) unsalted butter
1 recipe Basic Piecrust (recipe on page 228) for a single crust pie

1. Place apple slices in mixing bowl, and toss with ½ cup sugar, lemon juice, and apple pie spice. Allow to sit for 15 minutes.

2. Melt butter in 12-inch cast iron or other ovenproof skillet over medium-high heat. Stir in remaining 1 cup sugar and cook, stirring frequently, for 6–8 minutes, or until syrup is a deep walnut brown. Remove the pan from the heat, and set aside.

3. Preheat the oven to 425°F. Drain apple slices, and arrange them, tightly packed in a decorative pattern, on top of caramel in the skillet. Place remaining apple slices on top of decorative base. Place the pan over medium-high heat, and press down on the apples as they begin to soften.

4. Using a bulb baster or soup ladle, draw up juices from apples and spoon juices over apples on the top. Do not stir apples. After 5 minutes, or when apples begin to soften, cover the pan, and cook apples for 10–15 minutes, or until apples are soft and liquid is thick. During this time continue to baste apples.

5. Take the pan off the heat, and form dough into a circle 1 inch larger than the circumference of the pan. Tuck ends around apples on the sides of the pan using the tip of a paring knife. Cut 6 (1-inch) slits in top of dough to allow for release of steam.

6. Bake tart for 20 minutes, or until pastry is golden and juices are thick. Remove the pan from the oven, and allow to cool for 10 minutes. Using a knife, loosen edges of the tart from the pan. Invert a serving plate over the pan and then, holding the pan and the plate together firmly, invert them. Lift off the pan. Replace any apples that might have stuck to the bottom of the pan on top of the tart. Serve warm or at room temperature.

Note: The tart can be baked up to 6 hours in advance, and kept at room temperature.

Each serving contains:

5 MG SODIUM | 467 calories | 179 calories from fat | 20 g fat | 12 g saturated fat | 3 g protein | 73 g carbohydrates

Apple pie spice is a combination of fragrant spices that are pre-blended, so you don't have to purchase all of them individually. You can make your own by combining ½ teaspoon cinnamon, ¼ teaspoon nutmeg, ⅛ teaspoon allspice, ⅛ teaspoon ground cardamom, and ¼ teaspoon ground cloves. Or, in a pinch, substitute cinnamon as the primary base, with a dash of any of the other spices you might have on hand.

Cherry Clafouti

Clafouti originated in the Limousin region of France. It is a very light dessert that combines fruit and a batter to produce a "cake" with a texture that is a cross between a popover and a custard. This is also a great dessert to serve at brunch, because the fruit is clearly the star.

Yield: 8 servings | **Active time:** 10 minutes | **Start to finish:** 40 minutes

> 1 cup granulated sugar, divided
> 6 tablespoons all-purpose flour
> 6 large eggs, at room temperature
> 2 cups whole milk
> 2 teaspoons pure vanilla extract
> 2 cups halved and pitted sweet cherries
> 2 tablespoons unsalted butter, cut into bits
> Vanilla ice cream (optional)

1. Preheat the oven to 400°F, and grease a 9 x 13-inch baking pan.
2. Reserve 3 tablespoons sugar; combine remaining sugar, flour, eggs, milk, and vanilla in a food processor fitted with the steel blade or in a blender. Process until smooth.
3. Arrange cherries in the prepared baking pan, and pour custard over them. Bake for 20–25 minutes, or until the top is puffed and springy to the touch. Remove the pan from the oven and increase the oven temperature to broil.
4. Sprinkle cake with remaining 3 tablespoons sugar, dot with butter, and broil clafouti under the broiler about 3 inches from the heat for 1 minute, or until it is browned. Serve immediately with ice cream, if using.

Note: The batter can be prepared up to 1 day in advance and refrigerated, tightly covered. Remix it well. Do not bake the cake until just prior to serving.

Each serving contains:

78 MG SODIUM | 258 calories | 79 calories from fat | 9 g fat | 4 g saturated fat | 8 g protein | 38 g carbohydrates

Variation:

- Any fruit that holds its shape and cooks in a relatively short amount of time is a candidate for this dessert. These include sliced plums, sliced peaches, sliced apricots, and blueberries.

While many egg custard recipes are baked at a low temperature to keep the eggs tender, soufflés and cakes like this one are baked hotter to create steam to make them rise.

Citrus Angel Food Cake

The tangy tastes of orange and lemon are consistent with the light, airy quality of angel food cake. This cake can serve as the base for many mixed fruit salads, as well as being delicious by itself; it's also a great low-sodium treat to dip into Classic Chocolate Fondue (recipe on page 210).

Yield: 8 servings | **Active time:** 25 minutes | **Start to finish:** 2½ hours

3/4 cup orange juice
2 tablespoons finely grated orange zest
2 tablespoons finely grated lemon zest
3/4 cup cake flour
3/4 cup granulated sugar, divided
10 large egg whites, at room temperature
1 teaspoon cream of tartar

1. Preheat the oven to 350°F. Rinse a tube pan and shake it over the sink to remove excess moisture, but do not wipe it dry.
2. Combine orange juice, orange zest, and lemon zest in a small, heavy saucepan and bring to a boil over medium heat. Reduce by 3/4, pour mixture into a soup bowl, and refrigerate until cool. Sift flour with 1/4 cup of sugar; set aside.
3. Place egg whites in a grease-free mixing bowl and beat at medium speed with an electric mixer until frothy. Add cream of tartar, raise the speed to high, and beat until soft peaks form. Add remaining sugar, 1 tablespoon at a time, and continue to beat until stiff peaks form and meringue is glossy. Lower the speed to low and beat in cooled orange juice mixture. Gently fold flour mixture into meringue and scrape batter into the tube pan.
4. Bake in the center of the oven for 40–45 minutes, then remove cake from the oven and invert cake onto the neck of a tall bottle for at least 1½ hours, or until cool. Run a knife or spatula around the outside of the pan to loosen cake and invert cake onto a serving plate.

Note: Cake can be prepared up to 1 day in advance and kept at room temperature, tightly covered with plastic.

Each serving contains:

69 MG SODIUM | 144 calories | 2 calories from fat | 0 g fat | 0 g saturated fat | 6 g protein | 30 g carbohydrates

Variation:
- Substitute lime zest for the lemon zest.

Eggs should always be at room temperature when you use them in baking, since the whites will not increase in volume properly if they are chilled. An easy way to ensure this is to place the eggs in a bowl of very hot tap water for 5 minutes before separating them.

Lemon Meringue Pie

The rich filling for this pie is actually a lemon curd made with butter, which I like far better than a simple custard. In fact, you can make just the lemon filling and use it as a topping for fresh fruit if you don't want to go to the trouble of making the whole pie.

Yield: 8 servings | **Active time:** 25 minutes | **Start to finish:** 3 hours, including 2 hours for cooling

> 1 Basic Piecrust (recipe on page 228) for a 9-inch single crust pie
> 1 lemon
> $\frac{1}{3}$ cup bottled lemon juice, or as needed
> 6 tablespoons ($\frac{3}{4}$ stick) unsalted butter, thinly sliced
> $1\frac{1}{4}$ cups granulated sugar, divided
> 3 large eggs, at room temperature
> 5 large egg whites, at room temperature
> $\frac{1}{2}$ teaspoon cream of tartar

1. Totally pre-bake the pie shell as described on page 229.
2. Grate zest from lemon, and squeeze juice from fruit into a measuring cup. Add enough bottled lemon juice to make $\frac{1}{2}$ cup.
3. Preheat the oven to 400°F. Combine lemon zest, lemon juice, butter, and $\frac{1}{2}$ cup sugar in a saucepan. Cook over medium heat, stirring frequently, until sugar dissolves and mixture comes to a simmer. While mixture heats, whisk eggs in a mixing bowl until thick and lemon colored. Whisk in hot lemon juice mixture, and return mixture to the saucepan. Heat over medium heat, whisking constantly, until mixture comes to a simmer and thickens. Scrape curd into pre-baked pie shell, and chill while you make meringue.
4. Place egg whites in a grease-free mixing bowl and beat at medium speed with an electric mixer until frothy. Add cream of tartar, raise the speed to high, and beat until soft peaks form. Add remaining sugar, 1 tablespoon at a time, and continue to beat until stiff peaks form and meringue is glossy.
5. Spread meringue on top of lemon curd to totally cover filling. Bake for 15 minutes, or until meringue is golden brown. Cool pie on a rack for at least 2 hours before serving.

Note: The pie shell can be baked and the lemon filling can be made up to 2 days in advance. Keep pie shell at room temperature and refrigerate filling.

Each serving contains:

64 MG SODIUM | 418 calories | 201 calories from fat | 22 g fat | 13 g saturated fat | 7 g protein | 50 g carbohydrates

Variation:

- Substitute lime juice and lime zest for the lemon juice and lemon zest.

When making the desserts in this chapter, you'll frequently end up with leftover egg yolks. Unless in addition to following a low-sodium diet you're also on a low-cholesterol diet, don't throw out the yolks. Remember that nothing goes to waste in the kitchen. You can substitute 2 egg yolks for 1 whole egg when making anything from scrambled eggs to the quiche recipes in Chapter 5.

Baked Lime Custards

Hot custards are a homey treat, and these can be made at any time of the year because they're based on readily accessible limes. They have a light texture, almost like a soufflé.

Yield: 6 servings | **Active time:** 15 minutes | **Start to finish:** 35 minutes

1 lime
3 tablespoons bottled lime juice, or more as needed
3 large eggs, at room temperature
$\frac{1}{2}$ cup granulated sugar, divided
2 tablespoons all-purpose flour
1 cup half-and-half
$\frac{1}{4}$ teaspoon cream of tartar
$\frac{1}{4}$ cup confectioners' sugar

1. Preheat the oven to 350°F, and put a large kettle of water up to boil over high heat. Grease 6 (6-ounce) custard cups, and place them in a 9 x 13-inch baking pan. Grate zest from lime, and squeeze juice into a measuring cup; add enough bottled lime juice to measure $\frac{1}{4}$ cup. Separate eggs.

2. Whisk egg yolks and $\frac{1}{3}$ cup sugar for 2 minutes, or until thick and light in color. Whisk in lime zest and flour, and then whisk in lime juice and half-and-half. Set aside.

3. Place egg whites in a grease-free mixing bowl and beat at medium speed with an electric mixer until frothy. Add cream of tartar, raise the speed to high, and beat until soft peaks form. Add remaining sugar, 1 tablespoon at a time, and continue to beat until stiff peaks form.

4. Fold yolk mixture into whites, and divide batter into the prepared cups. Place the pan in the oven, and add boiling water to reach halfway up the sides of the custard cups.

5. Bake for 20–25 minutes, or until puddings are puffed and lightly browned. Dust tops of custards with confectioners' sugar, and serve immediately.

Note: The custards can be baked up to 4 hours in advance and served at room temperature; however, they will deflate. Do not dust with confectioners' sugar until just prior to serving.

Each serving contains:

52 MG SODIUM | 187 calories | 64 calories from fat | 7 g fat | 4 g saturated fat | 5 g protein | 27.5 g carbohydrates

Variation:
- Substitute lemon zest and lemon juice for the lime zest and lime juice.

Confectioners' sugar contains a small amount of cornstarch, which acts as a binding agent. If you make whipped cream with confectioners' sugar it will not separate as easily as cream beaten with granulated sugar.

Classic Chocolate Fondue

As a chocoholic, to me this gooey, rich fondue is the ultimate dessert! And there are so many low-sodium items you can use as dippers.

Yield: 8 servings | **Active time:** 15 minutes | **Start to finish:** 15 minutes

½ cup heavy cream

10 ounces bittersweet chocolate, chopped

2-3 tablespoons liquor or liqueur (your favorite: rum, bourbon, tequila, Cognac, brandy, triple sec, Grand Marnier, Chambord, kirsch, amaretto, Frangelico, crème de cacao, crème de banana, Irish cream liqueur, Kahlúa)

1. Combine cream and chocolate in a heavy 1-quart saucepan. Stir over very low heat to melt chocolate. When mixture is smooth and the chocolate is melted, stir in liquor.

2. Transfer fondue to a fondue pot or other pot with a heat source, and serve with banana chunks, apple slices, hulled strawberries, dried apricots, peach slices, or angel food cake cubes.

Note: The fondue can be prepared up to 4 hours in advance and kept at room temperature. Reheat it over very low heat, stirring frequently, or in a microwave oven.

Each serving contains:

6 MG SODIUM | 243 calories | 174 calories from fat | 19 g fat | 12 g saturated fat | 2 g protein | 19 g carbohydrates

Variation:

- If you're serving the fondue to children or adults who cannot tolerate alcohol, you can substitute ¼–½ teaspoon pure vanilla or almond extract plus 2 tablespoons water for the liquor or liqueur.

One of the health benefits of chocolate is that it has been found to contain catechins—some of the same antioxidants found in green tea. The catechins attack free radicals, which damage cells and are thought to lead to cancer and heart disease. So eating chocolate may help to prevent heart disease and cancer—as long as it's eaten in small quantities.

Almond Macaroons

I was thrilled to discover that almond paste, made from ground almonds and not much else, is a low-sodium product. These macaroons are very quick and easy to make, and when served in Italy they're topped with pine nuts.

Yield: 3 dozen | **Active time:** 15 minutes | **Start to finish:** 40 minutes

> 1 (8-ounce) can almond paste
> 1¼ cups granulated sugar
> 2 large egg whites
> ¾ cup pine nuts

1. Preheat the oven to 325°F, and grease 2 baking sheets.
2. Break almond paste into small pieces and place it in a mixing bowl along with sugar. Beat at medium speed with an electric mixer until combined. Increase the speed to high, add egg whites, and beat until mixture is light and fluffy.
3. Drop heaping tablespoons of dough onto the prepared baking sheets. Pat pine nuts into tops of cookies.
4. Bake cookies for 18–20 minutes, or until lightly browned. Place baking sheets on wire racks, and cool completely.

Note: The cookies can be made up to 5 days in advance and kept at room temperature in an airtight container.

Each 1-cookie serving contains:

4 MG SODIUM | 76 calories | 33 calories from fat | 4 g fat | 0 g saturated fat | 1 g protein | 10 g carbohydrates

Variation:

- Substitute chopped blanched almonds or chopped walnuts for the pine nuts.

> Make sure when buying the almond paste that it's almond paste and not marzipan, which is already sweetened and does contain sodium.

Chocolate Angel Food Cake

Light and airy angel food cake takes very well to being flavored with cocoa powder; it delivers a lot of chocolate flavor for very few calories, too. Top this cake with fruit salad for a more indulgent treat.

Yield: 8 servings | **Active time:** 20 minutes | **Start to finish:** 2½ hours

> 5 tablespoons unsweetened cocoa powder (not Dutch processed)
> ¾ cup cake flour
> ¾ cup granulated sugar, divided
> 10 large egg whites, at room temperature
> ¾ teaspoon cream of tartar
> 1 teaspoon pure vanilla extract

1. Preheat the oven to 350°F. Rinse out a tube pan and shake it over the sink, but do not wipe it dry. Set aside.
2. Sift together cocoa, flour, and ¼ cup of sugar. Set aside.
3. Place egg whites in a grease-free bowl and beat at medium speed with an electric mixer until frothy. Add cream of tartar and continue beating, raising the speed to high, until soft peaks form. Continue beating, adding remaining sugar, 1 tablespoon at a time, until meringue forms stiff peaks and is shiny. With the mixer at the lowest speed, beat in vanilla. Gently fold cocoa mixture into egg whites, being careful to avoid streaks of white meringue. Scrape batter into the tube pan.
4. Bake in the center of the oven for 40–45 minutes. Remove cake from the oven and invert the pan onto the neck of a tall bottle for at least 1½ hours, or until cool. Run a knife or spatula around the outside of the pan to loosen cake and invert cake onto a serving plate.

Note: Cake can be prepared up to 1 day in advance and kept at room temperature, tightly covered with plastic wrap.

Each serving contains:

70 MG SODIUM | 149 calories | 5 calories from fat | 1 g fat | 0 g saturated fat | 6 g protein | 31 g carbohydrates

Variations:
- Dissolve 1 tablespoon instant espresso powder in 2 tablespoons boiling water, and beat it into batter along with the vanilla for a mocha cake.
- Substitute pure almond extract for the vanilla, and add ³⁄₄ teaspoon ground cinnamon to the batter.

> While some brands of Dutch processed cocoa, which has a milder flavor than plain cocoa, are as low in sodium as the non-Dutch cocoa, other commercial brands are loaded with sodium. It's just easier to avoid them.

Warm Chocolate Tortes

These are my favorite dessert for a dinner party because they look so showy and they are quite easy to make. The center of each individual baked custard is a ball similar to a chocolate truffle, so it melts as the custard bakes and oozes out when cut. In a word, yum.

Yield: 6 servings | **Active time:** 20 minutes | **Start to finish:** 35 minutes

> 5 ounces bittersweet chocolate, chopped, divided
> 2 tablespoons heavy cream
> 1 tablespoon rum or fruit-flavored liqueur
> 5 tablespoons unsalted butter
> 2 large eggs
> 1 large egg yolk
> ¼ cup granulated sugar
> ¼ cup all-purpose flour
> Sweetened whipped cream or ice cream (optional)

1. Grease 6 muffin tins. Melt 2 ounces chocolate with cream and rum in a small microwave-safe dish. Stir well and refrigerate to harden. Form chocolate into 6 balls and refrigerate until ready to use.
2. Preheat the oven to 350°F.
3. Melt remaining chocolate with butter and allow to cool. Place eggs, egg yolk, and sugar in a medium mixing bowl. Beat with an electric mixer at medium and then high speed until very thick and triple in volume. Fold cooled chocolate into eggs, then fold in flour.
4. Divide batter among the prepared muffin tins and push a chocolate ball into the center of each tin. Bake tortes for 10–12 minutes, or until the sides are set. Remove the pan from the oven and invert onto a baking sheet. Serve immediately with whipped cream or ice cream, if using.

Note: The tortes can be prepared up to 2 hours before baking them, and the chocolate centers can be prepared up to 3 days in advance.

Each serving contains:

63 MG SODIUM | 347 calories | 230 calories from fat | 26 g fat | 14 g saturated fat | 8 g protein | 26 g carbohydrates

Variation:

- Add 1 teaspoon instant espresso powder to the chocolate and cream mixture.

Like fine wine, dark chocolate actually improves with age. Store it tightly wrapped in a cool place. Even if the chocolate has developed a gray "bloom" from being stored at too high a temperature, it is still fine to use for cooking.

Lemon Squares

I've been making these cookies with a crisp crust and creamy lemon topping since I was a child, and they remain at the top of my list. This is also a great last-minute recipe since most of us have a lemon or two in the house, along with basic baking ingredients.

Yield: 12 bars | **Active time:** 15 minutes | **Start to finish:** 1¼ hours

    1 lemon
    ¼ cup bottled lemon juice, or as needed
    ½ cup (1 stick) unsalted butter, melted
    ¼ cup confectioners' sugar
    1 cup plus 2 tablespoons all-purpose flour
    2 large eggs
    1 cup granulated sugar

1. Preheat the oven to 350°F. Grate zest from lemon, and squeeze juice from fruit. Add enough additional bottled lemon juice to make ⅓ cup. Set aside.

2. Combine butter, confectioners' sugar, and 1 cup flour in a mixing bowl, and mix thoroughly with a wooden spoon. Press mixture into an 8-inch square pan. Bake for 20 minutes, or until set and lightly brown. Remove crust from the oven, and set aside.

3. Combine eggs, granulated sugar, remaining 2 tablespoons flour, lemon juice, and lemon zest in a mixing bowl. Beat with an electric mixer on medium speed for 1 minute, or until well blended. Pour topping over crust and bake for 20 minutes, or until barely brown. The custard should still be soft. Cool the pan on a cooling rack, then cut into 12 pieces.

Note: These cookies can be refrigerated for up to 1 week, tightly covered.

Each 1 bar serving contains:

13 MG SODIUM | 202 calories | 78 calories from fat | 9 g fat | 5 g saturated fat | 2.5 g protein | 30 g carbohydrates

Variation:

- Substitute lime juice and lime zest for the lemon juice and lemon zest.

Chocolate Chip Blondies

Blondies are brown sugar–based shortbread dough baked into bar cookies, and these low-sodium sweets appeal to children of all ages, including big children called adults. Take them on a picnic, or pack them for lunch too.

Yield: 2 dozen | **Active time:** 15 minutes | **Start to finish:** 55 minutes

¼ pound (1 stick) unsalted butter, softened
1⅓ cups firmly packed light brown sugar
1 teaspoon pure vanilla extract
2 large eggs, at room temperature
1 cup all-purpose flour
1 cup semi-sweet chocolate chips

1. Preheat the oven to 350°F, and grease an 8 x 8-inch square pan.
2. Combine butter, sugar, and vanilla in a mixing bowl, and beat at medium speed with an electric mixer until blended. Increase the speed to high, and beat until light and fluffy. Beat in eggs, one at a time, beating well between each addition. Reduce the speed to low, and add flour. Fold in chocolate chips. Spread dough into the prepared pan.
3. Bake for 40 minutes, or until a toothpick inserted in the center comes out clean. Cool completely in the pan on a wire rack, then cut into 24 pieces.

Note: The cookies can be made up to 5 days in advance and kept at room temperature in an airtight container.

Each 1-cookie serving contains:

11 MG SODIUM | 140 calories | 58 calories from fat | 6.5 g fat | 4 g saturated fat | 1 g protein | 21 g carbohydrates

Variation:
• Substitute ½ cup walnuts for ½ cup of the chocolate chips.

Ginger Shortbread Slivers

Shortbread is a classic English cookie that is full of buttery flavor, and in this case the crisp cookies are enlivened with a bit of crystallized ginger. These are perfect cookies to serve with a fruit salad for dessert.

Yield: 16 cookies | **Active time:** 15 minutes | **Start to finish:** 45 minutes

1/4 pound (1 stick) unsalted butter, softened

3/4 cup granulated sugar

1 teaspoon pure vanilla extract

1 cup all-purpose flour

3 tablespoons cornstarch

1/4 cup finely chopped crystallized ginger

1. Preheat the oven to 350°F, and grease a 10-inch pie plate.
2. Combine butter, sugar, and vanilla in a mixing bowl, and beat at medium speed with an electric mixer until blended. Increase the speed to high, and beat until light and fluffy. Reduce the speed to low, and add flour, cornstarch, and ginger.
3. Press dough into the prepared pie plate, extending the sides up 1/2 inch. Cut dough into 16 thin wedges. Prick surface of dough all over with the tines of a fork.
4. Bake for 30 minutes, or until dough is lightly browned at the edges. Remove the pan from the oven, and go over cut lines again. Cool completely on a wire rack, and then remove slivers from the pie plate with a small spatula.

Note: The cookies can be made up to 5 days in advance and kept at room temperature in an airtight container.

Each 1-cookie serving contains:

1 MG SODIUM | 128 calories | 52 calories from fat | 6 g fat | 4 g saturated fat | 1 g protein | 18 g carbohydrates

Variations:

- Substitute 1/2 cup miniature chocolate chips for the ginger.
- Substitute 1/2 cup slivered almonds, toasted in a 350°F oven for 5–7 minutes, or until lightly browned, for the ginger, and substitute pure almond extract for the vanilla extract.

- Substitute ½ cup dried cranberries for the ginger, and add 1 tablespoon grated orange zest to the dough.
- Add 1 teaspoon apple pie spice and beat it along with the butter and sugar, and substitute ½ cup raisins for the ginger.

If you're in a hurry to begin a batter you can grate the butter through the large holes of a box grater. But do not soften butter in a microwave oven. It will become too soft.

Chocolate Chip Refrigerator Cookies

These crisp cookies are another old-fashioned favorite that are great to serve with healthful fruit salad or indulgent ice cream. The luscious flavor of the butter really comes through.

Yield: 4 dozen cookies | **Active time:** 15 minutes | **Start to finish:** 1½ hours, including 1 hour for chilling dough

> ¾ cup (1½ sticks) unsalted butter, softened
> ½ cup granulated sugar
> ¾ teaspoon pure vanilla extract
> 2 large egg yolks
> 1¾ cups all-purpose flour
> 1 cup miniature chocolate chips

1. Combine butter, sugar, and vanilla in a mixing bowl, and beat at medium speed with an electric mixer until blended. Increase the speed to high, and beat until light and fluffy. Reduce the speed to medium and add egg yolks, beating well and scraping the sides of the bowl as necessary. Reduce the speed to low, and add flour. Stir in chocolate chips.

2. Scrape dough onto a floured counter, and divide it in half. Roll each ½ into a log 2 inches in diameter. Wrap logs in plastic wrap, and refrigerate for 1 hour, or until chilled and firm.

3. Preheat the oven to 350°F and grease 2 cookie sheets. Slice logs into ¼-inch slices, and place them 1 inch apart on the prepared baking sheets. Bake cookies for 12–15 minutes, or until edges are lightly browned.

4. Remove the cookies from the oven and transfer to racks to cool completely.

Note: The cookies can be made up to 5 days in advance and kept at room temperature in an airtight container. Also, the logs can be refrigerated for up to 3 days or frozen for up to 3 months.

Each 1-cookie serving contains:

1 MG SODIUM | 70 calories | 38 calories from fat | 4 g fat | 2.5 g saturated fat | 1 g protein | 8 g carbohydrates

Variations:

- Substitute firmly packed dark brown sugar for the granulated sugar.
- Add 1/2 teaspoon ground cinnamon or ground ginger to the dough.

Never substitute chopped chocolate for chocolate chips. The chips are made with an emulsifier that holds them together as they bake, while chopped chocolate will melt into the batter.

Mocha Balls

Whoever invented the glorious combination of chocolate and coffee for a flavor dubbed mocha should have a special place in the panoply of cooks. If you're a mocha fan, then these cookies are for you.

Yield: 3 dozen | **Active time:** 20 minutes | **Start to finish:** 45 minutes

> 1 tablespoon instant espresso powder
> 2 tablespoons boiling water
> 8 tablespoons (1 stick) unsalted butter, softened and cut into small pieces
> 1/3 cup granulated sugar
> 1 large egg
> 1/2 teaspoon pure vanilla extract
> 3 tablespoons unsweetened cocoa powder (not Dutch processed)
> 1 1/3 cups all-purpose flour
> 1 cup confectioners' sugar

1. Preheat the oven to 350°F, and grease 2 baking sheets. Combine coffee powder and water in a small bowl, and stir well to dissolve coffee. Set aside.

2. Combine butter and sugar in a mixing bowl, and beat at medium speed with an electric mixer until light and fluffy. Add egg and vanilla, and beat well. Add cocoa powder and coffee mixture, and beat well, scraping the sides of the bowl as necessary. Reduce the speed to low, and add flour. Beat until just combined.

3. Form dough into 1-inch balls, and place them 1 inch apart on the prepared baking sheets. Bake for 15–18 minutes, or until firm. Remove the pans from the oven.

4. Sift confectioners' sugar into a low bowl, and add a few cookies at a time, rolling them around in the sugar to coat them well. Transfer cookies to a rack to cool completely.

Note: The cookies can be made up to 5 days in advance and kept at room temperature in an airtight container.

Each 1-cookie serving contains:

3 MG SODIUM | 60 calories | 25 calories from fat | 3 g fat | 2 g saturated fat | 1 g protein | 8 g carbohydrates

Variations:
- For coffee cookies, increase the instant espresso powder to 2 tablespoons and omit the cocoa.
- For a truly intensely flavored cookie, increase the instant espresso powder to 1½ tablespoons, and increase the cocoa to ¼ cup.

Instant espresso powder is imported from Italy, and it's now becoming more common to find in the U.S. It's made from real espresso coffee, which is then dehydrated and ground. Look for it in the supermarket along with other instant coffees.

Cream Puffs

The dough for this dessert is called *pâté a choux* in classic French cooking, and it's a useful dough to learn how to bake. You can make big cream puffs or small puffs; they can be sweet and filled with ice cream or pastry cream, or they can be savory and served as hors d'oeuvres stuffed with a cold filling.

Yield: 12 puffs | **Active time:** 20 minutes | **Start to finish:** 1¼ hours

1 cup water
6 tablespoons (¾ stick) unsalted butter
2 tablespoons granulated sugar
¼ teaspoon pure vanilla extract
¾ cup all-purpose flour
5 large eggs, divided

1. Preheat the oven to 425°F, and grease 2 cookie sheets.
2. Combine water, butter, sugar, and vanilla in a small saucepan, and bring to a boil over medium-high heat, stirring occasionally. Remove the pan from the heat, and add flour all at once. Using a wooden paddle or wide wooden spoon, beat flour into the liquid until it is smooth. Then place the saucepan over high heat and beat mixture constantly for 1–2 minutes, until it forms a mass that leaves the sides of the pan and begins to film the bottom of the pot.
3. Transfer mixture to a food processor fitted with the steel blade. Add 4 of the eggs, 1 at a time, beating well and scraping the sides of the work bowl between each addition . This can also be done by hand.
4. Scrape dough into a pastry bag. Make mounds of dough 2½ inches wide and 1 inch high. Or pipe mixture into lines of these dimensions for éclair shape.
5. Beat remaining egg, and brush only tops of dough mounds with a small pastry brush or rub gently with a finger dipped in the egg wash. (Be careful not to drip egg wash onto the baking sheet or egg may prevent dough from puffing.)
6. Bake at 425°F for 20 minutes, and then reduce the heat to 375°F and bake for an additional 10–15 minutes. Remove the pans from the oven and split puffs using a serrated knife. Turn off the oven and place baked puffs back into the oven with the oven door ajar for 10 minutes to finish crisping. Cool puffs in halves rather than whole, and pull out any dough from the center of the puffs that might be soggy.

Note: The puffs can be made up to 1 day in advance and kept at room temperature.

Each 1-puff serving contains:

31 MG SODIUM | 118 calories | 71 calories from fat | 8 g fat | 4 g saturated fat | 3.5 g protein | 8 g carbohydrates

Variations:
- For a cream puff ring, called Paris Breast in classic French cooking: Flour the greased baking sheet, and draw a 10-inch circle on the baking sheet, using a pot lid or platter as a guide. Pipe two thick lines side by side, using the circle as a guide, and then nestle one line into the crevice between the two. Bake for 20 minutes at 425°F, and then 25 minutes at 350°F. Split, pull out the damp dough, and crisp as described above.
- For small puffs, pipe mounds 1 inch in diameter and ½ inch high onto the baking sheets. Bake small puffs for 20–25 minutes, or until puffs are golden brown and crusty to the touch. Remove them from the oven and place on a wire rack to cool. This recipe makes 3 dozen small puffs.
- For puffs to serve filled with savory foods, omit the sugar and vanilla.
- For a classic French hors d'oeuvre called Gougères, omit the sugar and vanilla, and fold ¾ cup grated Swiss cheese into the dough. Bake as small puffs.

> If puffs become soggy, they can be crisped by placing them in a 350°F oven for 5–7 minutes. For large puffs, crisp the halves apart with the cut side up on both halves.

Pastry Cream

This pastry cream can be used to fill cream puffs or as a topping for any simple cake, or you can use it to top fresh fruit.

Yield: 2 cups | **Active time:** 15 minutes | **Start to finish:** 45 minutes

1½ cups whole milk, divided
4 large egg yolks
½ cup granulated sugar
¼ cup cornstarch
1 teaspoon pure vanilla extract

1. Combine ½ cup milk, egg yolks, sugar, cornstarch, and vanilla in a mixing bowl. Whisk for 2 minutes, or until mixture is thick and lemon colored.
2. While whisking yolk mixture, heat remaining 1 cup milk to a simmer in a saucepan over medium heat.
3. Slowly whisk hot milk into yolk mixture, and then pour mixture back into the saucepan. Cook over medium heat, whisking constantly, until mixture comes to a simmer and thickens. Remove the pan from the heat, and whisk until smooth.
4. Scrape pastry cream into a mixing bowl, and press a sheet of plastic wrap directly into the surface to prevent a skin from forming. Refrigerate for at least 30 minutes, or until cold.

Note: The pastry cream can be made up to 2 days in advance and refrigerated, tightly covered.

Each ¼-cup serving contains:

23 MG SODIUM | 120 calories | 34 calories from fat | 4 g fat | 2 g saturated fat | 3 g protein | 18 g carbohydrates

Variations:
- Add 3 tablespoons unsweetened cocoa (not Dutch processed) and 3 ounces bittersweet chocolate, chopped, to the milk as it heats. Make sure chocolate is dissolved and milk is smooth before adding it to yolk mixture.
- For mocha pastry cream, add 1–2 tablespoons instant espresso powder to the milk being heated. This is in addition to the cocoa and chocolate.

- Soak ½ cup raisins in ¼ cup rum for 30 minutes. Stir raisins and rum into pastry cream after it has finished cooking.
- Substitute 2 tablespoons orange juice concentrate or lemonade concentrate for 2 tablespoons of the milk being heated.

When adding hot liquids to the bowl while whisking, it helps to stabilize your bowl by rolling a kitchen towel up into a log, wrapping it into a coil as wide as the bowl's base, and setting the bowl onto it to nest it in place.

Basic Piecrust

One bakery item that's easy to make as a low-sodium food is piecrust, and even if you never make a traditional pie, knowing how to make pie crust is important. It could lead to spicy empanadas or a savory quiche for lunch. Piecrust is essentially flour and fat, mixed with a little water. The method remains constant; what changes is the proportion of ingredients.

Yield: Varies | **Active time:** 15 minutes | **Start to finish:** 15 minutes

Proportions for Piecrust

Size	All-Purpose Flour	Unsalted Butter	Ice Water
8–10-inch single	1 1/3 cups	1/2 cup	3–4 tablespoons
8–9-inch double	2 cups	3/4 cup	5–6 tablespoons
10-inch double	2 2/3 cups	1 cup	7–8 tablespoons

1. Place flour in a mixing bowl. Cut butter into cubes the size of lima beans, and cut into flour using a pastry blender, two knives, or your fingertips until mixture forms pea-sized chunks. This can also be done in a food processor fitted with the steel blade using on-and-off pulsing.

2. Sprinkle mixture with water, 1 tablespoon at a time. Toss lightly with fork until dough forms a ball. If using a food processor, process until mixture holds together when pressed between two fingers; if it is processed until it forms a ball, too much water has been added.

3. Depending on if it is to be a 1- or 2-crust pie, form dough into 1 or 2 (5–6-inch) "pancakes." Flour "pancake" lightly on both sides, and, if time permits, refrigerate dough before rolling it to allow more even distribution of the moisture.

4. Roll dough either between 2 sheets of waxed paper or inside a lightly floured jumbo plastic bag. Use the former method for piecrust dough that will be used for formed pastries such as empanadas, and the latter to make circles suitable for lining or topping a pie pan. For a round circle, make sure dough starts out in the center of the bag, and then keep turning it in 1/4 turns until the circle is 1 inch larger in diameter than the inverted pie plate. Either remove the top sheet of

wax paper or cut the bag open on the sides. You can either begin to cut out shapes or invert the dough into a pie plate, pressing it into the bottom and up the sides, and extending the dough 1 inch beyond the edge of the pie plate.

5. If you want to partially or totally bake pie shell before adding a filling, prick bottom and sides with a fork, press in a sheet of waxed paper or aluminum foil, and fill the pie plate with dried beans, rice, or the metal pie stones sold in cookware stores. Bake crust in a 375°F oven for 10–15 minutes. The shell is now partially baked. To complete baking, remove the weights and wax paper, and bake an additional 15–20 minutes, or until golden brown. Otherwise, fill pie shell. If you want a double crust pie, roll out the second dough "pancake" the same way you did the first half, and invert it over the top, crimping the edges and cutting in some steam vents with the tip of a sharp knife.

Note: The crust can be prepared up to 3 days in advance and refrigerated, tightly covered. Also, both dough "pancakes" and rolled out sheets can be frozen for up to 3 months.

8–10-inch single	8–9-inch double	10-inch double
Makes 8 servings	**Makes 8 servings**	**Makes 10 servings**
Each serving contains:	Each serving contains:	Each serving contains:
2 MG SODIUM	**3 MG SODIUM**	**3.5 MG SODIUM**
177 calories	266 calories	284 calories
105 calories from fat	158 calories from fat	169 calories from fat
12 g fat	18 g fat	19 g fat
7 g saturated fat	11 g saturated fat	12 g saturated fat
2 g protein	3 g protein	4 g protein
16 g carbohydrates	24 g carbohydrates	25.5 g carbohydrates

Variations:

- To create a fluted edge: Trim the pastry 1/2 inch beyond the edge of the plate, and fold under to make a plump pastry edge. Place your index finger on the inside of the pastry edge, right thumb and index finger on the outside. Pinch the pastry into V shapes, and repeat the pinching to sharpen the design.

- For an easy lattice crust: Cut ½–¾-inch wide strips of piecrust, using a pastry wheel or knife. Lay the strips across the pie in one direction, then in the other. Do not weave; however, fold edge of the bottom crust over the pastry strips and flute.
- For a shiny crust: Blend 1 egg yolk with 1 tablespoon milk or water. Brush over the top of the pie before baking.

Appendix A:
Metric Conversion Tables

The scientifically precise calculations needed for baking are not necessary when cooking conventionally. The tables in this appendix are designed for general cooking. If making conversions for baking, grab your calculator and compute the exact figure.

CONVERTING OUNCES TO GRAMS

The numbers in the following table are approximate. To reach the exact quantity of grams, multiply the number of ounces by 28.35.

Ounces	Grams
1 ounce	30 grams
2 ounces	60 grams
3 ounces	85 grams
4 ounces	115 grams
5 ounces	140 grams
6 ounces	180 grams
7 ounces	200 grams
8 ounces	225 grams
9 ounces	250 grams
10 ounces	285 grams
11 ounces	300 grams
12 ounces	340 grams
13 ounces	370 grams
14 ounces	400 grams
15 ounces	425 grams
16 ounces	450 grams

CONVERTING QUARTS TO LITERS

The numbers in the following table are approximate. To reach the exact amount of liters, multiply the number of quarts by 0.95.

Quarts	Liters
1 cup (1/4 quart)	1/4 liter
1 pint (1/2 quart)	1/2 liter
1 quart	1 liter
2 quarts	2 liters
2 1/2 quarts	2 1/2 liters
3 quarts	2 3/4 liters
4 quarts	3 3/4 liters
5 quarts	4 3/4 liters
6 quarts	5 1/2 liters
7 quarts	6 1/2 liters
8 quarts	7 1/2 liters

CONVERTING POUNDS TO GRAMS AND KILOGRAMS

The numbers in the following table are approximate. To reach the exact quantity of grams, multiply the number of pounds by 453.6.

Pounds	Grams; Kilograms
1 pound	450 grams
1 1/2 pounds	675 grams
2 pounds	900 grams
2 1/2 pounds	1,125 grams; 1 1/4 kilograms
3 pounds	1,350 grams
3 1/2 pounds	1,500 grams; 1 1/2 kilograms
4 pounds	1,800 grams
4 1/2 pounds	2 kilograms
5 pounds	2 1/4 kilograms
5 1/2 pounds	2 1/2 kilograms
6 pounds	2 3/4 kilograms
6 1/2 pounds	3 kilograms
7 pounds	3 1/4 kilograms
7 1/2 pounds	3 1/2 kilograms
8 pounds	3 3/4 kilograms

CONVERTING FAHRENHEIT TO CELSIUS

The numbers in the following table are approximate. To reach the exact temperature, subtract 32 from the Fahrenheit reading, multiply the number by 5, and then divide by 9.

Degrees Fahrenheit	Degrees Celsius
170°F	77°C
180°F	82°C
190°F	88°C
200°F	95°C
225°F	110°C
250°F	120°C
300°F	150°C
325°F	165°C
350°F	180°C
375°F	190°C
400°F	205°C
425°F	220°C
450°F	230°C
475°F	245°C
500°F	260°C

CONVERTING INCHES TO CENTIMETERS

The numbers in the following table are approximate. To reach the exact number of centimeters, multiply the number of inches by 2.54.

Inches	Centimeters
½ inch	1.5 centimeters
1 inch	2.5 centimeters
2 inches	5 centimeters
3 inches	8 centimeters
4 inches	10 centimeters
5 inches	13 centimeters
6 inches	15 centimeters
7 inches	18 centimeters
8 inches	20 centimeters
9 inches	23 centimeters
10 inches	25 centimeters
11 inches	28 centimeters
12 inches	30 centimeters

Table of Weights and Measures of Common Ingredients

Food	Quantity	Yield
Apples	1 pound	2½–3 cups sliced
Avocado	1 pound	1 cup mashed
Bananas	1 medium	1 cup sliced
Bell peppers	1 pound	3–4 cups sliced
Blueberries	1 pound	3⅓ cups
Butter	¼ pound (1 stick)	8 tablespoons
Cabbage	1 pound	4 cups packed shredded
Carrots	1 pound	3 cups diced or sliced
Chocolate, morsels	12 ounces	2 cups
Chocolate, bulk	1 ounce	3 tablespoons grated
Cocoa powder	1 ounce	¼ cup
Coconut, flaked	7 ounces	2½ cups
Cream	½ pint (1 cup)	2 cups whipped
Cream cheese	8 ounces	1 cup
Flour	1 pound	4 cups
Lemons	1 medium	3 tablespoons juice
Lemons	1 medium	2 teaspoons zest
Milk	1 quart	4 cups
Molasses	12 ounces	1½ cups
Mushrooms	1 pound	5 cups sliced
Onions	1 medium	½ cup chopped
Peaches	1 pound	2 cups sliced
Peanuts	5 ounces	1 cup
Pecans	6 ounces	1½ cups
Pineapple	1 medium	3 cups diced
Potatoes	1 pound	3 cups sliced
Raisins	1 pound	3 cups
Rice	1 pound	2 to 2½ cups raw
Spinach	1 pound	¾ cup cooked
Squash, summer	1 pound	3½ cups sliced
Strawberries	1 pint	1½ cups sliced

Food	Quantity	Yield
Sugar, brown	1 pound	2$\frac{1}{4}$ cups, packed
Sugar, confectioners'	1 pound	4 cups
Sugar, granulated	1 pound	2$\frac{1}{4}$ cups
Tomatoes	1 pound	1$\frac{1}{2}$ cups pulp
Walnuts	4 ounces	1 cup

TABLE OF LIQUID MEASUREMENTS

Dash	=	less than $\frac{1}{8}$ teaspoon
3 teaspoons	=	1 tablespoon
2 tablespoons	=	1 ounce
8 tablespoons	=	$\frac{1}{2}$ cup
2 cups	=	1 pint
1 quart	=	2 pints
1 gallon	=	4 quarts

Index